Kingfish to America

KINGFISH TO AMERICA:

Edited and
with an Introduction
by Henry M. Christman

Share Our Wealth

SELECTED SENATORIAL PAPERS OF

Huey P. Long

SCHOCKEN BOOKS • New York

First published by Schocken Books 1985
10 9 8 7 6 5 4 3 2 1   85 86 87 88
Copyright © 1985 by Henry M. Christman

Library of Congress Cataloging in Publication Data
Long, Huey Pierce, 1893–1935.
    Kingfish to America, share our wealth.
    Includes index.
    1. Populism—United States—Addresses, essays,
lectures. 2. United States—Politics and government—
1933–1945—Addresses, essays, lectures. 3. United
States—Economic policy—1933–1945—Addresses, essays,
lectures. 4. Long, Huey Pierce, 1893–1935.
I. Christman, Henry M. II. Title.
E742.L662   1985   973.917   85–2392

Design by Nancy Dale Muldoon
Manufactured in the United States of America
ISBN 0–8052–3998–7

Contents

Introduction

> And it is here, under this oak where Evangeline waited for her lover, Gabriel, who never came. This oak is an immortal spot, made so by Longfellow's poem, but Evangeline is not the only one who has waited here in disappointment. Where are the schools that you have waited for your children to have, that have never come? Where are the roads and the highways that you send your money to build, that are no nearer now than ever before? Where are the institutions to care for the sick and the disabled? Evangeline wept bitter tears in her disappointment, but it lasted through only one lifetime. Your tears in this country, around this oak, have lasted for generations. Give me the chance to dry the tears of those who still weep here!
>
> —*Huey P. Long, in an address at St. Martinville, Louisiana, 1927*

This was the vision of Huey Pierce Long, then Chairman of the Louisiana Public Service Commission and candidate for the Democratic nomination for Governor of Louisiana.

As Governor, Long transformed Louisiana through a reform of state services unprecedented and unique in American history: A vast public works program of new highways, roads, and bridges; increased appropriations for education from primary school through university, with the introduction of free textbooks for all schoolchildren, and free night schools for adults; upgraded public health care, including free hospital services; and reform of state public services across the board.

Governor Long of Louisiana subsequently became United States Senator Long in January 1932; and Governor Franklin D. Roosevelt of New York became President Roosevelt the following year.

These two brilliant, charismatic men, with such contrasting personalities, originally allies in the progressive cause, were to become bitter, implacable foes, and proponents of rival programs and philosophies.

Long's program of national reform died with him in 1935, and has been forgotten, while Roosevelt's program of national reform was enacted as the New Deal, and changed the history of the United States.

America, and the world, know of Roosevelt's New Deal; few have heard of Long's Share Our Wealth.

This small volume makes available Long's national philosophy and national program, in his own words, for reexamination and reconsideration a half-century later, on the fiftieth anniversary of Long's formulation and proclamation of his Share Our Wealth program.

The interests of justice, of historical truth, require that Long be judged impartially on the basis of what he actually did say and actually did advocate.

Justice and history further require that Long's ideas be readily available because of their relevance to contemporary economic, social, and political issues and problems.

This volume is in no sense a Long autobiography assembled through his papers. Nor is it in any sense a biography; that need has been splendidly fulfilled by the distinguished scholar, the late T. Harry Williams, Boyd Professor of History at Louisiana State University, in his Pulitzer prize-winning biography, *Huey Long,* a classic of its kind.

Of course, Long hoped that his Share Our Wealth program and movement would carry him into the White House. And his critics charged that this was the exclusive purpose and sole significance of Share Our Wealth—an opportunistic and even crackpot scheme and vehicle that Long himself did not take seriously. But Long's flamboyant personality and manners, his controversial "political machine" tactics and associations, and even his rhetoric itself aided his opponents.

In certain key respects, Long was an updated William Jennings Bryan. Indeed, it was from Bryan that Long acquired his famous slogan, "Every Man a King!" Bryan's complete phrase was: "Behold a Republic: Whose every man is a King, but no one wears a crown." Like Bryan, Long was an agrarian Populist; like Bryan, he was a charismatic, mesmerizing orator; and, like Bryan, he constantly invoked the Bible.

Long's Bible-brandishing, country-drummer style, with intentionally bad grammar, rustic anecdotes, simplistic examples and explanations, presented in coarse, vulgar, and frequently obscene language, appalled and repelled cultured persons.

It is noteworthy that Long's speaking style was developed not through traditional education and/or conventional communications training and experience, but rather through his observation of and experience with country people as a traveling salesman.

What we today would term Long's public relations "image" problem was compounded by his simultaneous roles in Louisiana as both a political insurgent and a social outsider. Long rejected Southern ante-bellum traditions and manners, either ignoring or dismissing outright the Confederate culture and heritage. And he meanwhile battled powerful and entrenched economic special interests, led by Standard Oil.

Consequently, Long carried to Washington a reputation already smeared by his enemies, and much of the press, as a wild, ignorant, uncouth, ruthless, communistic, demented Southern redneck.

In January 1932, Long entered a Senate led by traditionalist Southern Democratic conservatives and reactionaries who despised him. Long's mentor and closest friend in that body was the revered Senator George Norris of Nebraska, perhaps the greatest, and certainly the most generally beloved progressive Republican of that era.

Despite his reputation, Long soon compelled serious and impar-

tial observers in Washington to view him in an entirely new light.
On April 4, 1932, Long stunned the Senate and the Washington
press corps with a sensational exposé, "The Doom of America's
Dream," which was described at the time as the most radical, most
bitter address ever delivered in the United States Senate.

This remarkable address is probably the outstanding example of
Long's unique ability to articulate the unarticulated suffering and
despair of the majority of Americans during the thirties. Long
boldly asserted that the United States faced violent revolution; he
darkly justified violence as a desperate last resort against depriva-
tion; and he demanded the forthwith redistribution of wealth.

The speech established Long as one of the most radical members of the United States Senate then, and perhaps ever. Significantly, although Long spoke only of economic and social conditions in America, his address prophetically analyzed the parallel
despair in Western Europe which led to the rise and victory of
Nazism and Fascism there.

Within a year, Long's break with Roosevelt was final. Roosevelt
had campaigned on the issue of redistribution of wealth, and Long
said Roosevelt had personally assured him that the commitment
would be kept. Accordingly, Long charged that Roosevelt not
only betrayed his campaign promises, but also his political and
personal pledges to Long.

In any case, rivalry between the New York aristocratic liberal
and the Louisiana plebian Populist was inevitable. As T. Harry
Williams states:

> Two great politicians had come into inevitable conflict. Each
> was so constituted that he had to dominate other and lesser
> men. Neither could yield to the other without submerging him-
> self and dimming his destiny. And instinctively each recognized
> the other's greatness, and feared it.

By early 1934, Long not only had distanced himself from Roosevelt politically and personally, but moved to challenge Roosevelt
with a rival program. On February 5, 1934, he specified the principles and goals of his Share Our Wealth program in his statement,
"Carry Out the Command of the Lord."

Long expanded further on this theme several weeks later in a half-hour national radio address, "Every Man a King," broadcast over the National Broadcasting System, the text of which he inserted in *The Congressional Record.*

Share Our Wealth would guarantee every American family a "homestead"—"a home, an automobile, a radio, and the ordinary conveniences"—and a basic annual income. In addition, there would be pensions for the aged, benefits for veterans, and assistance for college students.

These benefits would be financed by a capital tax that would place an absolute limit on fortunes, and an income tax that would place an absolute limit on annual incomes.

Other features of Share Our Wealth included a proposal to "share the work" by limiting the hours and months of labor for every American worker, thereby creating additional jobs.

The Share Our Wealth movement was informally and loosely organized, without national dues, so membership figures are not precise. By any standard, however, the general public response to Long was enormous; it is said that his offices received more than 7½ million letters and postcards, this at a time when the population of the nation was not much more than half that of today's America—and when the price of a stamp was a substantial expenditure for many.

Long dramatized his break with Roosevelt through a series of national radio addresses during the first half of 1935. These were slashing, sarcastic attacks with such titles as, "Our Plundering Government," "Our Blundering Government," and "The St. Vitus' Dance Government."

In his last major campaign in the Senate, Long championed the cause of veterans' benefits, a burning issue of the day which, ironically, brought public attention at different times to both of the persons Roosevelt considered to be the two most dangerous men in America—on the left, Long; and on the right, a rising young military officer, Douglas MacArthur, who already had attained notoriety for his heartless dispersal of impoverished veterans in Washington.

The remarkable career of Huey Pierce Long came to an abrupt

close when he was shot in Baton Rouge on September 9, 1935, and died there the next day.

In his brief career, Long provoked such hatred from his enemies that some of them would meet and draw lots to determine which should be the one to kill him. It was, therefore, a final irony that Long was gunned down not by some berserk political foe, or through some conspiracy, but by a quiet young physician, Dr. Carl Weiss, acting alone.

Long served in the Senate for less than four years; and during much of this time he was in Louisiana, battling his political foes and extending his reform program through his domination of state government.

Only twice was Long successful in electing other Democratic Senators. In Louisiana, the aristocratic John H. Overton unseated Senator Edwin Broussard, thereby giving Long a threefold victory: Deposing a key foe; elevating Long to senior Senator from Louisiana; and bringing him a loyal and scholarly junior colleague. In neighboring Arkansas, Long came to the aid of Senator Hattie Caraway, a quiet widow who had been appointed as a compromise choice to fill the unexpired term of her deceased husband, and unexpectedly sought to retain the seat on her own. The "Huey and Hattie" madcap campaign across Arkansas created a sensation, and scored a stunning upset victory.

With such a short tenure as a freshman senator, Long's senatorial record is inevitably brief. Ostracized from the beginning by the Senate's conservative Southern Democratic establishment, Long faced additional antagonism from New Deal Democrats following his break with Roosevelt. An outcast, Long had little opportunity to pass bills. Probably his greatest legislative victory was the enactment of government insurance of bank deposits.

Long's crucial contribution to the work of the Senate was to speed passage of New Deal legislation by the constant threat of bolder proposals that would steal Roosevelt's political thunder.

Long demonstrated great courage not only by defying the powerful Roosevelt Administration from the Democratic Party Left, but also in holding fast to his principles throughout his career, even when he had little to gain and much to lose.

He was a consistent and faithful friend of organized labor in Baton Rouge and in Washington, even though the labor vote in Louisiana at the time was negligible. Significantly, Long's original law practice and specialty was Workmen's Compensation.

He was a pioneering defender of both civil liberties and civil rights. Long rejected loyalty oaths for all Louisiana public employees—civil servants, teachers, and professors alike. He was outspoken in his defense of academic freedom for professors, courageously asserting, "All the radicals and reds in the colleges won't do any harm. It's a mighty good thing that they are beginning to do a little thinking. I wish there were a few million radicals."

Even more courageous was his unrelenting opposition to the Ku Klux Klan. Probably Long's most colorful skirmish with the Klan was in 1934, when the head of the KKK announced that he was going to Louisiana to campaign against Long. Long responded with a press conference in which he denounced the Klan leader in unprintable terms, concluding that if the "Imperial bastard" entered Louisiana, he would leave with "his toes turned up." The KKK leader canceled his proposed trip.

Especially poignant was Long's characterization of Nazism: "I don't know much about Hitler. Except this last thing, about the Jews. There has never been a country that put its heel down on the Jews that ever lived afterwards."

Most of all, Long was passionately dedicated to economic justice for all. This was his true cause, his overriding concern and commitment; his every word, every proposal, every action, conformed to, and with, that goal.

From the perspective of a half-century, it can be said that Huey Pierce Long made two major contributions to American history.

First: Long forced Roosevelt to the left, thereby expanding the scope of the New Deal and hastening its enactment.

This aspect of Long's record is established and documented with great distinction by T. Harry Williams in his biography of Long.

Even before his break with Roosevelt, Long was a relentless critic of what he perceived to be both the general and the specific deficiencies and flaws of New Deal measures.

Long correctly understood that the New Deal public works projects, which he termed the "dole roll," would not by themselves alter the economic imbalances and injustices of the nation. "You are giving the little man a biscuit to eat, and you put a barrel of flour more taxes on top of his head to carry," he roared in the Senate.

When Roosevelt ultimately was compelled to respond to Long's Share Our Wealth program with a New Deal plan to redistribute wealth through graduated income taxes, a triumphant Long taunted a subdued Senate, concluding, "I just wish to say 'Amen'," as he endorsed Roosevelt's proposal.

Roosevelt's emulation of Long's Share Our Wealth ideas did not escape public notice. The nationally beloved humorist, Will Rogers, wrote of Roosevelt's graduated income tax program: "I would sure liked to have seen Huey's face when he was woke up in the middle of the night by the President, who said 'Lay over, Huey, I want to get in bed with you'."

Long had further sport in the Senate with Rogers's quip. But Long's characteristic role was to expose the shortcomings of the New Deal. For example, when he learned that the forthcoming Social Security program would be financed not by general revenue, but instead would be a system of intergenerational transfers paid by workers through payroll taxes, Long was caustic: ". . .the poor people who get relief will pay for it. In other words, the poor people will be allowed to help the poor people, a poor wage-earner will be allowed to help his aged father or mother and take away a little more from his wife and children. Ain't that grand?"

Second: Long's Share Our Wealth program was a radical, genuine, practical Left alternative to Roosevelt's New Deal.

Admittedly, Long did not work out all the details of his program, nor did he live to have the opportunity to do so.

Long's style of speaking mostly or entirely extemporaneously, tailoring his material to the audience and responding to their reactions, affects the unity and coherence of his material. Long could develop an entire address and speak for hours with only a few notes scribbled on the back of an envelope.

However, from the perspective of history a half-century later, the basic goal of Long's Share Our Wealth program—that all citizens be guaranteed the fundamental necessities of life, paid for by graduated taxes in a democratic society—is not a utopian vision or a crackpot fantasy. Independently of Long and the United States, this social welfare society has been a reality of daily life for decades in Northern Europe, where the social welfare reforms of the thirties far surpassed the reforms of America's New Deal.

Significantly, Long followed his announcement of the Share Our Wealth program with a journey from Washington to New York, in order to debate Norman Thomas, the famed Socialist leader and spokesman. In this remarkable debate, Thomas asserted the traditional Socialist program of democratic control of the means of production, in opposition to Long's program of redistribution of wealth through taxation. Prophetically, this Thomas–Long debate anticipated the subsequent historic differences of philosophies and programs of, on one hand, the British Labour Party, which advocated extensive nationalization of basic industries, and, on the other, of the Swedish Social Democratic Party, which proposed leaving all industries almost entirely in private hands, but highly regulated and heavily taxed. (Long, by the way, charmed his sophisticated New York audience, which mobbed him with requests for his autograph.)

Most certainly, Huey Pierce Long was a dominant and domineering personality. He was incredibly creative; indeed, he created himself, working himself up from poverty and obscurity, battling against arrogant and unyielding citadels of power and privilege. He encountered ruthless tactics, and responded in kind.

Revered by his supporters and reviled by his opponents, Long was denounced by his enemies as the "Caesar of the bayous," the "despot of the delta," and worse; all of which one journalist dubbed "Kingfishophobia."

In retrospect, Long seems larger than life; and he has passed into legend. But the controversial, sensational aspects of his life and career have too often overshadowed and obscured and even eclipsed his very substantial achievements and contributions.

Long did not live to fulfill his ultimate ambition, to have occasion to use the song he already had written for his prospective Presidential campaign:

Why weep or slumber, America?
  Land of brave and true
With castles, clothing and food for all
  All belongs to you
Ev'ry man a king, ev'ry man a king.

The social welfare society that Long envisioned for America was not accomplished then, nor has it been accomplished now, fifty years later. Even so, Long left a unique record of achievement at the state level, implementing public works, public education, and public health reforms; a unique record of protest at the national level, of speaking out against suffering and injustice; and a uniquely original program at the national level, intended to relieve that suffering and right that injustice.

Long dreamed of, and passionately advocated, a more democratic, more progressive, more just, more compassionate, more perfect society, with dignity, basic economic security, and economic and cultural opportunities for all—a better life and a better world that he described "in the radiance of the future."

As Franklin Delano Roosevelt of New York and his New Deal deserve to live and do live enshrined in history, Huey Pierce Long of Louisiana and his share–our–wealth program should be accorded their just places in the history of America and the memory of humankind.

                                        Henry M. Christman

Franklin Delano Roosevelt Drive
New York, New York

The Doom of America's Dream

THE CONGRESSIONAL RECORD
April 4, 1932

Mr. Long. Mr. President, the Senator from Michigan [Mr. Couzens] takes a little exception to the statement made by the Senator from Arkansas [Mr. Robinson*], on this side of the Chamber, relative to the reduction of salaries of Federal employees. In the discussion which has been going on here in this Chamber there is really a little bit too much harmony; in fact, this is about 95 percent the most harmonious discussion to which I have ever listened.

It seems that the Senator from Arkansas [Mr. Robinson] and the Senator speaking for the administration [Mr. Vandenberg†] are in accord that taxes should be saved the American taxpayer through whatever eliminations can be made at this time.

I see this morning, in one of the daily papers published here in Washington, that it is reported that a bipartisan drive is on among the leaders of the Senate. It says:

---

*Joseph T. Robinson, Democratic Senator from Arkansas, Democratic Minority Leader when Long entered the Senate, and subsequently Democratic Majority Leader.

†Arthur H. Vandenberg, Republican Senator from Michigan from 1928 until his death in 1951; originally a prominent isolationist, he subsequently led the internationalist wing of the Republican Party in support of Roosevelt and Truman bipartisan foreign policy.

What worries Senate leaders is a fear that the so-called tariff taxes adopted by the House, such as levies on oil and coal, will lead to a bitter fight that will delay the bill. An effort, therefore, will be made to eliminate these taxes and substitute other levies to make up the loss.

As I said here on the floor of the Senate less than a month ago, when the balancing of the Budget reaches the point where there is going to be a tax on the Standard Oil Co., then it is going to become necessary to find other levies; and if you do not find other levies, then the demand is going to come here in the Senate to reduce salaries and wages of the employees of the Federal Government.

The Rich Men's Club

I do not speak alone for the men drawing $1,200 a year nor for the men drawing $1,500 a year. I speak for the men drawing $10,000 a year, sitting in the Senate and in the House of Representatives. I say that there is not a man here who can stand the campaign expenses connected with election to the United States Senate and live six years on what he gets in the United States Senate; and to reduce the salaries of Congressmen and Senators today is not tending in any direction whatever except to make this body a rich men's club.

We know that there was a coalition over in the House on this tax bill, and on the raising of revenue for the Government. The newspapers tell us that there is a coalition in the Senate. I want to know if there is a coalition in the Senate on this tax bill; if so, whom it is between, where it was made up, where they met, who blessed the conference, and who was at the anointing, if there has been a coalition, conference, agreement, or tentative agreement or effort to agree on this tax bill. They tell us it was so in the House, and the leaders said it was so. The publications of the United States condemned every man in the House who did not fall in line behind one or the other of the party leaders.

Bloated Fortunes

Of course, there is need of money for the Government. What are we to get? That is not the main need of this country, Mr. President. The reason why the Government needs money, the reason why industry needs money, comes from an infernal condition of concentration of wealth; and never has any of these bipartisan conferences in either one of the Houses of Congress recommended anything being done along the line of the redistribution of wealth here in the United States to avoid the alarming condition that we are in now.

Oh, no; something must be done to balance the Budget; but Mr. [Herbert] Hoover comes in when the time gets about ripe, and you can read his messages between the lines, and you do not have to eat a whole beef to tell when it is tainted— he comes in about the time when there arises the spirit in either one of these Houses to put these taxes where they ought to be put, and changes the estimates of the requirements of the Budget to suit the peculiar conditions and circumstances arising at that time. If the House looks like it is going to become rebellious in raising the funds, they report that there is a mistake of $500 million in the Budget. Then the matter subsides, and the House becomes docile. Then they demand that other remedies be taken to balance the Budget.

O Mr. President and Members of the Senate, there never was a more determined fight than is being waged today— silently, under cover, behind the silken veil, and out in front—to keep this tax bill from going into the field of surtaxes and inheritance taxes, that would give the common man of this country a chance, and to give the wealth of this country an opportunity to be distributed among the people of the United States.

What is the tax bill going to contain when it comes out? We have waited a long time to get some help. If it has already

been agreed upon, let us know now from the party leaders, as
they gave it out in the House. Let us know in the Senate. Why
wait? Is there going to be any relief for the masses of this
country in this tax bill? Let us know what is going to come.

On this home by horror haunted—tell me truly, I implore:
Is there—is there balm in Gilead? Tell me—tell me, I implore!

What is to be the balm from the tax bill? What is to be the
balm?

America's Crisis

Why, if this Congress adjourns and does not provide a law
for the effective starting of a redistribution of wealth in the
United States you need not be worried about the amount of
deficit that there is going to be in the National Treasury. If
we adjourn here with this tax bill before us, with a bill
passed as a result of it or with this bill passed, without providing a means for the redistribution of wealth in the United
States today, and allow this snowball to go downhill for two
or three more years as it is now, and allow this panic to be
exploited as it is now being exploited to concentrate every
business enterprise in this country, you do not need to worry
about the Federal Government nor the Budget of the Federal Government. You will have a problem before you that
is a great deal bigger than any problem of the Budget of the
Federal Government.

I have letters which I have received today, which I intended to read to the Senate. One man, a peaceable citizen,
has undertaken to make a living as long as he could, and
finally went into a business prohibited by law because it was
the only thing out of which he could make a living for his
wife and children. He is now in the Federal penitentiary.
Another letter is from a widow with a 19-year-old son that
she is undertaking to send to college, living in a college
town; and he cannot continue his work in the university
because she can not find the funds even to buy the books.
Yet we are sitting here talking about balancing the Budget.

The Unblessed Coalition

Who is thinking about those people? Who is thinking about this condition? Who is doing anything about it? Where is this bipartisan conference? I want to find it and write it a letter. Has it been blessed as the House conference was blessed? Have Rockefeller and Morgan and Baruch sent in their ill-fated recommendations and demands that were so effective in other administrations? Have they been sent in now? Is that what we are going to see done in this tax bill that is coming out here?

We are told that there never was a ruling class that abdicated. A great deal of speculation is made over who is the leader and who are the party leaders of this Nation, who are the leaders of Congress. I have been here long enough to say that if I had any legislation in the United States Congress to-day, I would a whole lot rather know that it had the sanction and approval of Morgan and Rockefeller and Baruch than to know that it had the sanction and approval of every party leader in both Houses of Congress. They are here to fight the tax on the importation of oil. They are here to fight the tax on stock exchanges.

We have a cotton exchange and a stock exchange in the city of New Orleans, just as they have a stock exchange and a cotton exchange in the city of New York, and I am not afraid to tell you that there is not a more nefarious enterprise that ever operated on the face of the globe than the stock exchanges and cotton exchanges in the city of New York and in the city of New Orleans. They have lived for years out of the miseries and the slim profits that might have meant some convenience and comfort to the people of this country, and there is no tax on the living face of the globe that can be more justly and properly assessed than a tax on the stock exchange and a tax on the cotton exchange. I am not politically afraid for them to know that I have expressed exactly those sentiments on the floor of the

Senate. It does not make any difference to me whether they like it or not.

Now, these men are fighting the inheritance tax and the surtax. The newspapers tell us that this is a great effort to soak the rich. Soak the rich—the "soak the rich campaign." It is no campaign to soak the rich, Mr. President. It is a campaign to save the rich. It is a campaign the success of which they will wish for when it is too late, it it fails, more than anyone else on earth will wish for it—a campaign for surtaxes to insure a redistribution of wealth and of income, a campaign for inheritance taxes to insure a redistribution of wealth and of income.

Is Wall Street Alone to Have the Coalition?

Since we had a coalition of the Republican and Democratic leaders in the House and in the Senate that the House Members rebelled against, is it not possible that there can be some coalition of the Members of the United States Senate in the interest of the people of this country to raise these surtaxes and these inheritance taxes and to save these other forms of taxation that mean a prosperous America? Could there not be some anointed move from the Senate that would mean the protection of the people of this country?

Evidently we do not realize that there is a crisis. Apparently we do not. We do not have to go very far to find it out. Mr. Herbert Hoover, in his speech in Indianapolis the other day, said that we were now in the midst of the greatest crisis in the history of the world. If Mr. Hoover can be believed, neither disunion, rebellion, war, nor pestilence compares with the condition that faces the American people today. Mr. Hoover may not ever say this again. I do not think he will say it again. I think he had a rather unguarded moment, and probably his speech was not censored as it is going to be censored in the future. As campaign days draw closer, the artist who can make words mean and not mean will no doubt interpolate these messages in such a way that they will offend but few, and benefit probably fewer. But Mr. Hoover went on to say that a different means of taxation had to be found for this country; that we had to find a means of taxation that would take the taxes off the small man. That is what Mr. Hoover said. I am going to read in a moment just exactly what he did say; that we had to formulate a tax policy that would take the taxes off the farmers and home owners of this country; and in the same speech—which evidently was not censored as most of them probably will be hereafter and probably have been heretofore—he went on and said that the remedy was by the distribution of wealth.

But now every power of the Administration which can be brought from the White House is exerted against anything being done which means the distribution of wealth among the people of this country.

The Light of America's Dream Is Fading

The great and grand dream of America that all men are created free and equal, endowed with the inalienable right of life and liberty and the pursuit of happiness—this great dream of America, this great light, and this great hope—has almost gone out of sight in this day and time, and everybody knows it; and there is a mere candle flicker here and yonder to take the place of what the great dream of America was supposed to be.

Another Slave Owner

The people of this country have fought and have struggled, trying, by one process and the other, to bring about the change that would save the American country to the ideal and purposes of America. They are met with the Democratic Party at one time and the Republican Party at another time, and both of them at another time, and nothing can be squeezed through these party organizations that goes far enough to bring the American people to a condition where they have such a thing as a livable country. We swapped the tyrant 3,000 miles away for a handful of financial slaveowning overlords who make the tyrant of Great Britain seem mild.

Much talk is indulged in to the effect that the great fortunes of the United States are sacred, that they have been built up by the honest and individual initiative, that the funds were honorably acquired by men of genius far-visioned in thought. The fact that those fortunes have been acquired and that those who have built them for the financial masters have become impoverished is a sufficient proof that they have not been regularly and honorably acquired in this country.

Even if they had been that would not alter the case. I find that the Morgan and Rockefeller groups alone held, together, 341 directorships in 112 banks, railroad, insurance, and other corporations, and one of this group made an after-dinner speech in which he said that a newspaper report had asserted that 12 men in the United States controlled the business of the Nation, and in the same speech to this group he said, "And I am one of the 12 and you the balance, and this statement is correct."

Twelve men! If we only had that passing remark, which, by the way, was deleted from the newspaper report which finally went out, although we have plenty of authority that the statement was made; if we did not have other figures to show it, we probably might not pay so much attention to that passing remark.

You want to enforce the law, you want to balance the Budget? I tell you that if in any country I live in, despite every physical and intellectual effort I could put forth. I should see my children starving and my wife starving, its laws against robbing and against stealing and against bootlegging would not amount to any more to me than they would to any other man when it came to a matter of facing the time of starvation.

Whoever tries to guard the existence of these fortunes becomes a statesman of high repute. He is welcome in the party counsels. Whoever undertakes to provide for the distribution of these fortunes is welcome in no counsel.

They pass laws under which people may be put in jail for utterances made in war times and other times, but you cannot stifle or keep from growing, as poverty and starvation and hunger increase in this country, the spirit of the American people, if there is going to be any spirit in America at all.

Let All Enjoy Our Wealth If the Country Is to Be Saved

Unless we provide for the redistribution of wealth in this country, the country is doomed; there is going to be no country left here very long. That may sound a little bit extravagant, but I tell you that we are not going to have this good little America here long if we do not take care to redistribute the wealth of this country.

Here is a report of the Federal Trade Commission published in 1926. On page 58 I find this:

> The foregoing table shows that about 1 per cent of the estimated number of decedents owned abut 59 per cent of the estimated wealth, and that more than 90 per cent was owned by about 13 per cent of this number.

That is the very conservative and highly subsidized Federal Trade Commission, which said that 1 percent of the decedents owned 59 percent of the wealth. It had been previously estimated, as I read the other day from the report of the Industrial Relations Committee, just 10 years before that time, that 2 percent of the people owned 60 percent of the wealth, and in 10 years the cycle grew, so that from one Government report the estimate that 2 percent of the people owned 60 percent of the wealth, in 10 years had become 1 percent of the people owning 59 percent of the wealth of this country. That is how that condition grew.

I have here an editorial which appeared in the *Saturday Evening Post* at the time this first report was published. This editorial appeared on September 23, 1916, in the *Saturday Evening Post* under the heading, Are We Rich or Poor? I read from the editorial, which is just a column:

> The man who studies wealth in the United States from statistics only will get nowhere with the subjects because all the statistics afford only an inconclusive suggestion. Along one statistical line—

This is the *Saturday Evening Post* in 1916 before its owner began to come to Washington in a $3,000,000 yacht. Says this editorial:

Along one statistical line you can figure out a nation bustling with wealth; along another a bloated plutocracy comprising 1 per cent of the population lording it over a starveling horde with only a thin margin of merely well-to-do in between.

That is from the *Saturday Evening Post* of September 23, 1916.

I saw an article in the *World's Work* for last month which gives the details of the Mellon fortune, and totals it up at seven billion nine hundred and ninety million four hundred and twenty-five thousand—that is enough without getting to the hundreds—seven billion nine hundred and ninety million. That is the Mellon fortune, with a footnote to the effect that it did not include two billion one hundred and sixty-six million his brother has. The Mellon fortune $10,000,000,000, and everybody knows that the Mellon fortune does not compare with the Rockefeller fortune. Thirty-two fortunes of the Mellon size would take every dime of property America has in it to-day. Thirty-two men! No wonder 12 men were in absolute control of the United States.

Who Owns America?

I have here the statistics showing the concentration of American industries.

IRON ORE: 50 to 75 percent owned by the United States Steel Corporation.

STEEL: 40 percent of the mill capacity owned by the United States Steel Corporation.

NICKEL: 90 percent owned by the International Nickel Co.

ALUMINUM: 100 percent owned by the Aluminum Trust.

TELEPHONE: 80 percent owned by the American Telephone & Telegraph Co. It is more than that, as they would state if they understood the subsidizing contract which that company requires every little independent telephone company to sign in order to get long-distance connections. If that were stated, it would be found that the telephone industry in the United States is 100 percent in the hands of the American Telephone & Telegraph Co.

TELEGRAPH: 75 percent in the Western Union.

PARLOR CAR: Pullman Co., 100 percent monopoly.

AGRICULTURAL MACHINERY: The International Harvester Co. has 50 percent.

SHOE MACHINERY: The United Shoe Machinery Co. has a monopoly.

SEWING MACHINES: The Singer Sewing Machine Co. controls that field.

RADIO: The Radio Corporation, 100 percent.

SUGAR: The American Sugar Refining Co., 100 percent.

ANTHRACITE COAL: Eight companies, 80 percent of the United States tonnage.

SULPHUR: Two companies own the world's deposits.

OIL: To show how conservative this report is, it states that 33 percent of the oil is controlled by five companies, when, as a matter of fact, they own 105 percent, if you can get that much out of the total quantity of oil produced. That which they do not own they have absolute dominion over and manipulate the oil tariffs and the importations of the foreign group in such a manner that no independent man can stay in the oil business in this country today in competition with the Standard Oil Co.

MEAT PACKING: Two companies, 50 percent.

ELECTRICAL EQUIPMENT: Two companies, 50 percent.

RAILROAD ROLLING STOCK: Two companies, monopoly.

CHEMICALS: Three companies, monopoly.

MATCHES: Two companies, monopoly.

RUBBER: Four companies, monopoly.

MOVING PICTURES: Three companies, monopoly.

AVIATION: Three companies, monopoly.

ELECTRIC POWER: Four groups, monopoly.

INSURANCE: Ten companies, 66 percent of the insurance in force.

BANKING: 1 percent of the banks control 99 percent of the banking resources of the United States.

That is the concentration that has occurred in this country. The statistics further show that only 2 percent of the

people ever pay income taxes. Mr. [Andrew W.] Mellon*
points out that that is a grave condition; that the law has
been miraculously at fault in failing to collect an income tax
against a larger percentage of the people.

It is not the law that is at fault. That is not the trouble at
all. It is the infernal fact that 98 percent of the people of the
United States have nothing, rather than it being the fault of
the fact that only 2 percent of them pay any income tax.

Mr. Mellon wants to broaden the tax, so he said in his
statement. He has gone to Europe by this time—at least we
hope so. Mr. Mellon said that he wants the law broadened so
as to cover more than 2 percent. That means that he wants to
go into the pockets of the little man living from hand to mouth
on the bank of some creek or in some little cabin with 40 acres
and a mule. That means that he wants to reach down lower
into the lower strata and take from the starvation wages of
that class of people so that he might relieve the upper crust
from paying the burdens of government.

I have here the address by President Hoover delivered at
Indianapolis. Here is what he said:

> Above all, schemes of public works which have no reproduc-
> tive value would result in sheer waste. Public works would result
> in sheer waste.
> The remedy to economic depression is not waste but the cre-
> ation and distribution of wealth.

"The creation and distribution of wealth." He said further
that in this creation and distribution taxes have got to be
lifted from the small man. Therefore, Mr. President, there is
necessity that something must be done in this crisis for the
benefit of the people of the country, as well as for the benefit
of balancing the Budget.

---

*Andrew W. Mellon, multi-millionaire banker and financier, served as Republi-
can Secretary of the Treasury from 1921 to 1932 under Presidents Harding, Cool-
idge, and Hoover.

Over 2,000,000 Earn Less Than 504 Plutocrats

I have the statistics here. Here is how the income is being distributed. In 1929 there were 504 supermillionaires at the top of the heap who had an aggregate net income of $1,185,000,000. That is 504 people. These 504 persons could have purchased with their net income the entire wheat and cotton crops of 1930. In other words, there were 504 men who made more money in that year than all the wheat farmers and all the cotton farmers in this great land of democracy. Out of the two chief crops, 1,300,000 wheat farmers and 1,032,000 cotton farmers—2,300,000 farmers raising wheat and cotton—made less than those 504 men.

From the official statistics we find that $538,664,187 was the net income of the 85 largest income-tax payers in 1929. The 421,000 workers in the clothing industry received in wages $475,000,000. Those 85 men could have paid the entire wages of the clothing industry of the Nation and have had $100 million left. Yes; there has got to be relief from this condition.

Mr. [Samuel] Gompers* was termed a socialist when he said:

> Hundreds of thousands of our fellow men, through the ever-increasing extensions and improvements in modern methods of production, are rendered superfluous. We must find employment for our wretched brothers and sisters by reducing hours of labor or we will be overwhelmed and destroyed.

That was his statement, but the statement that the country faced any such thing as destruction was heralded as a preposterous statement, but Mr. Hoover came back and clarified the matter. He did not disturb Mr. Gompers's ashes, because they are underneath the earth all alone. Mr. Hoover

*Samuel Gompers, founder and first president of the American Federation of Labor.

came back and went Mr. Gompers one better. He said this is "the greatest crisis the world has ever known."

I have here a newspaper article in the nature of an interview with the Senator from Michigan [Mr. COUZENS]. I want to read a line from that. This was published in the *St. Louis Post-Dispatch* of May 27, 1931: "Senator JAMES COUZENS (Michigan) does not believe the depression in this country is due to world depression." And I do not either. "Nor does he believe that our recovery depends upon world recovery." Nor do I. "He believes, and emphatically says, that American capitalists caused the American depression mainly by taking an exorbitant share of the earnings of American industry, and that recovery can be accomplished only by securing the livelihoods and increasing the purchasing power of American workers."

All Agreed "No Swollen Fortunes"

I have here an article appearing in the *Saturday Evening Post* on the question of the distribution of wealth of this country. Whenever fear comes around, as it did in 1919, there was a fear that Bolshevism was going to overrun this country like it threatened to overrun Europe. Then we get such expressions as this. We cannot get them at any other time. Here was the *Saturday Evening Post,* the great conservative journal, saying this: "We want prosperity in America, but not swollen fortunes."

That is the *Saturday Evening Post* saying that we do not want "swollen fortunes in America." Then it went on to say: "We want big rewards for men who do big constructive things, and jail sentences for the big fellows who steal the fruits of their work and the savings of small investors."

They wanted to put Rockefeller and Morgan in jail, according to this editorial; but today the cry is, "Soak the rich," and the man who undertakes to levy a penny on the concentrated bloated fortunes in the hands of a few of them is considered an outlaw.

"There have been altogether too many mavericks loose on the range, sucking cows on which they have no claim. There would be no real railroad mess, no necessity for trying to pare down wages in basic industries—"

The same thing prevailed then that prevails now, the same condition practically, and the *Saturday Evening Post* said: "There would be no real railroad mess, no necessity for trying to pare down wages in basic industries, if there had been no banker control and no flagrant watering of the stocks of these corporations."

That was the *Saturday Evening Post* in 1919. It said, "We want prosperity, but no swollen fortunes," and that the men who have made most of those swollen fortunes by impoverishing the labor of the country ought to be put in jail. We are not trying to put them in jail. We are trying to save them from committing physical suicide in this country and pulling the temple down with everybody else in it.

But we have a coalition! We have a coalition of the Democratic Party leaders and the Republican Party leaders. Yes; we have a coalition. Who are the anointed of this coalition of Democratic and Republican leaders that is going to eliminate everything that means protection of the common men in this country? Where is this coalition? Where does it meet? With whom does it meet? Has it ever for once come out before the American people with anything except the statement that they have to hold the House in order? Will they come out with the same declaration that they have got to hold the Senate in order—not trying to do anything particularly, but only holding everything in order? The House is described as "being in rebellion" when it rebels against its leaders.

Is there going to be one coalition? Is that going to be the extent? Are there not men enough in the Senate of the United States who will see to it that there is a coalition for the people of the United States? Is there not some way there can be a coalition that takes into consideration the man with the house full of starving children, or has there got to be only one coalition to protect the banker control, which it was said, as I have pointed out, ought to have been in the penitentiary 20 years ago? What is to be the coalition?

The pastor of Mr. John D. Rockefeller's church had something to say about it. I do not suppose he will ever say it again. They probably did not get to look over this speech of his in advance. If they had done so, it would possibly have been different. There would have been a different interpretation of it and they would have had more interpolations in it. Here is what Mr. Rockefeller's pastor said on December 28, 1930: "See the picture of the world to-day—communism rising as a prodigious world power and all the capitalistic nations arming themselves to the teeth to fly at each other's throats and tear each other to pieces. . . . Capitalism is on trial. . . . Our whole capitalistic society is on trial."

I should say it is on trial—not the capitalistic system, but the lack of capital.

Then Mr. Rockefeller's pastor proceeded: "First, within itself, for obviously there is something the matter with the operation of a system that over the western world leaves millions and millions of people out of work who want work, and millions more in the sinister shadow of poverty."

There is bound to be something wrong with the system. Then he proceeds: "Second, capitalism is on trial, with communism for its world competitor."

And it is. "The verbal damning of communism now prevalently popular in the United States will get us nowhere. The decision between capitalism and communism hinges on one point: Can capitalism adjust itself to the new age?"

The Example of Marie Antoinette

When the poor people of France cried for bread, Marie Antoinette said, "If they have no bread let them eat cake." They reared back and took the head of the King and the Queen. Today Marie Antoinette has been outdone forty times over. The poor people have pleaded for jobs, for the right to work; they have pleaded for a living; they have pleaded for their homes; they have pleaded for clothes to wear; they have pleaded for food to eat. There are plenty of homes; there is ample food; there is everything that is needed for humanity; but instead of saying, "If you have not bread eat cake," the American people witness a so-called bipartisan agreement that, under the claim of "balancing the Budget," reaches down and puts a tax upon people crying to this Government for relief.

Mr. John Dewey proceeds to say that there has got to be a redistribution.

Here is a quotation from the dean of the Harvard Graduate School of Business Administration, Wallace B. Donham: "If we have not in our several countries the brains, ability, and the cooperative spirit necessary to cure such world-wide conditions as those in which we now find ourselves, then our mass production, our scientific progress, our control over nature may actually destroy civilization."

And that is what is going to happen. Machines are created making it possible to manufacture more in an hour than used to be manufactured in a month; more is produced by the labor of one man than was formerly produced by the labor of a thousand men; fertilizers are available whereby an acre of land can be made to produce from two to three or even four times what it formerly produced; various other inventions and scientific achievements which God has seen fit to disclose to man from time to time make their appearance; but instead of bringing prosperity, ease, and comfort, they have meant unemployment; they have meant idleness; they have meant starvation; they have meant pestilence; whereas they should have meant that hours of labor were shortened, that toil was decreased, that more people would be able to consume, that they would have time for pleasure, time for recreation—in fact, everything that could have been done by science and invention and wealth and progress in this country should have been shared among the people.

Refunding Millions to the Wealthy

Mr. President, the senior Senator from Arkansas, our Democratic leader, whom I respect very highly and whom I honor for the great service which he has done to this country, saw fit to join in the clamor for the reduction of wages. I maintain there is no need of reducing any wages. Anyone should have seen the trouble which was coming when former Senator James A. Reed, of Missouri, rose on this floor when the tax bill of 1926 was under consideration in the Senate and said that the Democratic Party had been betrayed by its leaders. I thought that statement was a bit beyond the proper or necessary limit at the time; but the surtax was manipulated downward and the drive went on.

The coalition between the progressive Senators and the Democrats managed to keep the surtaxes not where they should have been, but nearer where they should have been than otherwise would have been the case. However, all of a sudden, the famous coalition occurred and the Duke's Mixture amendment went through here. It might have done North Carolina some good; it might have done some good to some college or colleges in North Carolina, but it was a means by which the Treasury paid out millions and millions and multiplied millions of funds. It was a retroactive amendment to open wide the gates of the Public Treasury and tell the capitalists to come and get not only what the Government was going to collect, but to come and get what they had already paid. So there were refunded out of the Public Treasury enormous amounts of money.

That was followed by the Mellon crusade to return and throw to the winds or to the public financial manipulators of this country hundreds of millions more of dollars. Then, Mr. President, they pared down the income-tax rates from 65 to 50, to 40, to 25, and down to 20 and the inheritance-tax rates were pared down in about the same manner and proportion, until now a bipartisan bill comes here, with all the blessings it ever had and a defunct Treasury as a result of it, concerning which ample warning was given at the time. A blind man could have seen what the country was being led into.

Over in the House there was proposed to the bill which has been sent here from that body an amendment known as the Swing amendment. It does not entirely, according to the estimate of the President and his departmental heads, provide enough taxes to balance the Budget, and, according to him, they want to make a few little changes, but to them it is pretty satisfactory. Surely it is satisfactory. They managed to sweat the rate down to a point where the bloated fortunes of this country will have to pay but very little more than they have been paying, and they made the whole measure temporary, in that it is to last only two years. Why only two years? Because the people of this country get strong enough about every 25 years to make a fight and get a break and enjoy a chance of doing anything, and if the proposed taxed legislation can be made at the end of two years ipso facto to cease, it is not going to amount to a snap of a finger. That provision is in the bill.

There have not been provided, as the public press or some portions of the public press have been led to believe any such inheritance taxes or surtaxes as we formerly had in this country. Proponents of the bill are trying to say that they are going back to wartime rates, but they are not going back to the wartime rates by a jugful. Their maximum is 40 percent. They stop increasing the latter upward, in the case of surtaxes, after $100,000 is reached. They do practically the same thing in the case of inheritances over a million dollars. The wartime rates, however, do not compare with what the rates ought to be now, because at the time of the World War 2 percent of the people owned 60 percent of the wealth, whereas in these times 1 percent of the people own 59 percent of the wealth. In wartime we had no such conditions as we have today, and we have the word of President Herbert Hoover to confirm that statement, that this is the greatest crisis the world has ever faced, in war times or any other times.

We had no such unemployment in wartime as we have today. We had no such hunger and starvation and idleness; we had no conditions to compare with those now existing; and so, instead of those rates being held down to the wartime basis, they should have been boosted far beyond that on the centralized wealth of this country in order to give the people a share of the profits being earned in the country today. But the rates have not even been made equal to those of the wartime. The wartime rates went up to 65 percent, while the rates in the bill now pending in the Senate stop at 40 percent.

Mr. President, I intended to close, but I want to make one more observation, briefly. I do not mean to criticize the courts of this country particularly. I mean to criticize the method by which the courts are composed. We are going to have to couple to tax legislation some antitrust legislation or write into the present antitrust law what the Congress originally wrote into it. The original Sherman antitrust law provided that any restraint of trade was a violation of the law; any monopoly, any conspiracy in restraint of trade was obnoxious to the law. When the question came before the Senate, on the floor of the Senate an effort was made to write into the bill that anything that "unreasonably" restrained trade would be prohibited, but the Senate and the Congress refused to write the nefarious so-called rule of reason into the antitrust law when it was passed.

Those who opposed the law came back to the Senate of the United States and tried to get it amended, but the Senate committee said we will not write the rule of reason in the law because it would destroy the antitrust law. So they went before the United States Supreme Court in Case No. 1, and the court held that there was no rule of reason in it, and the common law did not apply; they went back in case No. 2, and the Supreme Court said, "The common law does not apply and any restraint of trade is prohibited." They went back in case No. 3, and the Supreme Court said, "We are surprised that anybody should urge this question again, but we now again tell you for the third time that any restraint of trade is prohibited, and there is no rule of reason in the law." They went back the fourth time, and the Supreme Court of the United States said the same thing; they went back the fifth time and the Supreme Court of the United States said the same thing; but, oh, my, suddenly one day the papers blazoned forth the news that President [William Howard] Taft had done a most liberal and constructive and monumental thing in naming a Democrat, a former Confederate soldier, Chief Justice of the United States, and there were plaudits over the appointment. A little later other judges were placed on the Supreme Court of the United States, and then the monopolists went back to the Supreme Court. The trust lawyers who had fought this law had been made the masters of the law by being put on the Supreme Court of the United States, and then, with the dish all cooked up, the motions were gone through again presenting the case to the United States Supreme Court after they had passed on it five straight times, and the United States Supreme Court wrote a long opinion through its Chief Justice, Mr. [Edward Douglass] White, from my native State of Louisiana, and said that "the rule of reason" had to be written into the Standard Oil case and the American Tobacco Co. case, and this country has virtually been without an antitrust law ever since.

Mr. William Jennings Bryan wrote a letter about this to Mr. Taft at the time.

William J. Bryan, three times Democratic candidate for President of the United States, openly charged Taft with packing the Supreme Court.

Mr. Bryan said to Mr. Taft—"You promised that you were going to amend the antitrust law in the presidential campaign of 1908, but you have got a Congress on your hands that will not permit its amendment, so you have appointed a Supreme Court—"

And President Taft made more appointments to that bench than any other President—"and you have secured that amendment to the antitrust law by the Supreme Court."

Mr. George W. Perkins, head of the Steel Trust, came out with a statement. I quote: "George W. Perkins, associated with J. P. Morgan in trust control, delivered a speech in which he complained that the Republican Congressmen had not tried to redeem their platform promise, but that it had been redeemed by the Supreme Court in the recent trust decision, wherein the rule of reason was applied."

In other words, they amended the law by the other legislative body that Mr. Taft had set up at the time—the Supreme Court of the United States—and that is not the only law that they have amended in that way; not by a jugful.

We had some jurisprudence against these public-service corporations. I appeared here before the United States Supreme Court in those cases, and before the other Federal courts in these cases. They involved the basis of value of a public-service corporation's property—whether it would be the actual prudent investment or whether it would be the so-called replacement value, less depreciation.

In the case of Smyth against Ames the Supreme Court of the United States had held that you had to consider the cost of the property and all other elements in determining the value of public-service property. In the case that I had, which, by the way, was a telephone case, the Circuit Court of Appeals—and they were upheld by the Supreme Court as far as they could go—held that that theory was still the law; that the cost and the replacement and all those elements had to be considered in determining the value of property; but they began to load down the court. The corporations began to pound, with all the anvils and with all the iron, that they should consider nothing except the cost of replacement of utility property, because they had all the engineers in the world. The ordinary city cannot fight a public-service-corporation case. It cost the State of Louisiana all the money it could rake and scrape to fight one telephone case, and the telephone company submitted a bill of costs of about $500,000 for fighting that case, and then charged it back into operating costs. The ordinary city cannot compete with the company's experts and technicians in cases of that kind. Finally, however, they loaded the Supreme Court down until the question was right before the court again; and in the Carrollton Railroad case, from the State of Georgia, as I remember, they came out again and said that they considered the cost of property and these replacements together in deciding its value. But then when they got another case up there, lo and behold, the skies opened, and they sent out to the Northwest and got a man and put him on the Supreme Court of the United States who had been doing more to bring about that doctrine of replacement value than any other man we knew of. He was made a member of the Supreme Court of the United States; and then they brought up the Indianapolis waterworks case, and they reversed the whole kit and boodle, and said that the dominant-cost theory must be on replacement.

That is how this matter has been manipulated. We have created boards and commissions, and we have courts. We have passed laws, and we have enacted various and sundry things, but we have never been able to create a commission that lasted very long. We have never been able to get a rule of law interpreted that stood for any particular time unless they began, by some contrivance or machination, to make the element that was affected by it the master of the law that was being enforced. They have become the masters of the law.

How long is it going to last? How long can it last? How long will it last? I tell you, Mr. President, it cannot last very long.

In conclusion, I am not asking any man in the United States Senate to do anything harmful to the rich people of this country. If you want to do them a favor, provide some way to put some of that wealth among some of the people of this country. If you want to make their lives secure, provide a way for relieving the anxieties of 90 percent of the people in this country today who are in absolute fear of want and impoverishment. Provide a way whereby the world is going to provide a living for the people of the United States, if you love these rich people as much as I love them. Yes, sir; provide a way to distribute it. If we sit here in this Congress and let this tax bill go back with a clause ipso facto annulling the law at the end of two years, so that these taxes will no longer be collected; if we do not raise these surtaxes and these inheritance taxes to a point where they cannot continue to perpetuate these massive fortunes in the United States, like a snowball going downhill; if we do not regulate them, when you have gone and gathered it all and all and all, in what condition are you going to leave the country? It is in it already. You do not have to go any farther. It is in it already. You mark my words: When we come back to the next meeting of the United States Senate, things are not going to be any better than they are right now, and not as good. You mark my words: You will look back on the year 1932 as a prosperous year in 1933.

You remember what I am saying. If we do not provide surtaxes and inheritance taxes to break up these large fortunes, and to provide for the needs of this Government from sources that are able to pay the cost, when we come back here in 1933 you are going to find a changed condition, and you will be wondering how conditions could have been as good in 1932 as they are now.

But Why Not the Dream of America?

But O Mr. President, if we could simply let the people enjoy the wealth and the accumulations and the earnings and the income and the machinery and the contrivances that we have. If, with the invention of every machine, we could secure the education of every man; if with increased production of every kind there could be less toil, more hours of pleasure and recreation; if there could be a happy and contented people enjoying what the Almighty has made it possible to provide; if there could be people clothed with the materials that we have to clothe them with today, and no place to put them; if the people could be fed with the food that we have to feed them with, and no place to put it; if the people could be sheltered in the homes we have today that the Federal land bank has taken away from them because they cannot pay the interest on the mortgages—if that could be done, if we could distribute this surplus wealth, while leaving these rich people all the luxuries they can possibly use, what a different world this would be.

"Thy Soul Shall Be Required"

Do not take away anything they need. Leave them with all the luxuries that the world can provide them for hundreds and hundreds and hundreds of years. Leave them with every palace, with every convenience, with every comfort; but do not allow the concentration and stagnation of wealth to reach the point where it is a national calamity.

Will we do that? Will they do it? No; we know they will not do it. Will we do it for them? Maybe we will. Maybe we will not. There ought to be a coalition of the people; there ought to be a coalition of the Senators representing the rights of the people in a situation of this kind, as efficient as is the coalition of the bipartisan movement recommending and sponsoring the other side of the field.

We can do this. If we do not, we will leave these masters of finance and fame and fortune like the man in the book of old, who said to himself, so the Bible tells us:

> I will pull down my barns, and build greater; and there will I bestow all my fruits and my goods.
>
> And I will say to my soul: Soul, thou hast much goods laid up for many years; take thine ease, eat, drink, and be merry.
>
> But God said unto him: Thou fool, this night thy soul shall be required of thee.

Carry Out the Command of the Lord

THE CONGRESSIONAL RECORD
February 5, 1934

MR. LONG. Mr. President, I send to the desk and ask to have printed in the RECORD not a speech but what is more in the nature of an appeal to the people of America.

There being no objection, the paper entitled "Carry Out the Command of the Lord" was ordered to be printed in the RECORD, as follows:

By Huey P. Long, United States Senator

People of America: In every community get together at once and organize a share-our-wealth society—Motto: Every man a king.

Principles and platform:

1. To limit poverty by providing that every deserving family shall share in the wealth of America for not less than one third of the average wealth, thereby to possess not less than $5,000 free of debt.

2. To limit fortunes to such a few million dollars as will allow the balance of the American people to share in the wealth and profits of the land.

3. Old-age pensions of $30 per month to persons over 60 years of age who do not earn as much as $1,000 per year or who possess less than $10,000 in cash or property, thereby to remove from the

field of labor in times of unemployment those who have contributed their share to the public service.

4. To limit the hours of work to such an extent as to prevent overproduction and to give the workers of America some share in the recreations, conveniences, and luxuries of life.

5. To balance agricultural production with what can be sold and consumed according to the laws of God, which have never failed.

6. To care for the veterans of our wars.

7. Taxation to run the Government to be supported, first, by reducing big fortunes from the top, thereby to improve the country and provide employment in public works whenever agricultural surplus is such as to render unnecessary, in whole or in part, any particular crop.

Simple and Concrete—Not an Experiment

To share our wealth by providing for every deserving family to have one third of the average wealth would mean that, at the worst, such a family could have a fairly comfortable home, an automobile, and a radio, with other reasonable home conveniences, and a place to educate their children. Through sharing the work, that is, by limiting the hours of toil so that all would share in what is made and produced in the land, every family would have enough coming in every year to feed, clothe, and provide a fair share of the luxuries of life to its members. Such is the result to a family, at the worst.

From the worst to the best there would be no limit to opportunity. One might become a millionaire or more. There would be a chance for talent to make a man big, because enough would be floating in the land to give brains its chance to be used. As it is, no matter how smart a man may be, everything is tied up in so few hands that no amount of energy or talent has a chance to gain any of it.

Would it break up big concerns? No. It would simply mean that, instead of one man getting all the one concern made, that there might be 1,000 or 10,000 persons sharing in such excess fortune, any one of whom, or all of whom, might be millionaires and over.

I ask somebody in every city, town, village, and farm community of America to take this as my personal request to call a meeting of as many neighbors and friends as will come to it to start a share-our-wealth society. Elect a president and a secretary and charge no dues. The meeting can be held at a courthouse, in some town hall or public building, or in the home of someone.

It does not matter how many will come to the first meeting. Get a society organized, if it has only two members. Then let us get to work quick, quick, quick to put an end by law to people starving and going naked in this land of too much to eat and too much to wear. The case is all with us. It is the word and work of the Lord. The Gideons had but two men when they organized. Three tailors of Tooley Street drew the Magna Carta of England. The Lord says: "For where two or three are gathered together in My name, there am I in the midst of them."

We propose to help our people into the place where the Lord said was their rightful own and no more.

We have waited long enough for these financial masters to do these things. They have promised and promised. Now we find our country $10 billion further in debt on account of the depression, and big lenders even propose to get 90 percent of that out of the hides of the common people in the form of a sales tax.

There is nothing wrong with the United States. We have more food than we can eat. We have more clothes and things out of which to make clothes than we can wear. We have more houses and lands than the whole 120 million can use if they all had good homes. So what is the trouble? Nothing except that a handful of men have everything and the balance of the people have nothing if their debts were paid. There should be every man a king in this land flowing with milk and honey instead of the lords of finance at the top and slaves and peasants at the bottom.

Now be prepared for the slurs and snickers of some high-ups when you start your local spread-our-wealth society. Also when you call your meeting be on your guard for some smart-aleck tool of the interests to come in and ask questions. Refer such to me for an answer to any question, and I will send you a copy. Spend your time getting the people to work to save their children and to save their homes, or to get a home for those who have already lost their own.

To explain the title, motto, and principles of such a society I give the full information, viz:

Title: Share-our-wealth society is simply to mean that God's creatures on this lovely American continent have a right to share in the wealth they have created in this country. They have the right to a living, with the conveniences and some of the luxuries of this life, so long as there are too many or enough for all. They have a right to raise their children in a healthy, wholesome atmosphere and to educate them, rather than to face the dread of their under-nourishment and sadness by being denied a real life.

Motto: "Every man a king" conveys the great plan of God and of the Declaration of Independence, which said: "All men are created equal." It conveys that no one man is the lord of another, but that from the head to the foot of every man is carried his sovereignty.

Now to cover the principles of the share-our-wealth society, I give them in order:

1. To limit poverty:

We propose that a deserving family shall share in our wealth of America at least for one third the average. An average family is slightly less than five persons. The number has become less during depression. The United States total wealth in normal times is about $400 billion or about $15,000 to a family. If there were fair distribution of our things in America, our national wealth would be three or four or five times the $400 billion, because a free, circulating wealth is worth many times more than wealth congested and frozen into a few hands as is America's wealth. But, figuring only on the basis of wealth as valued when frozen into a few hands, there is the average of $15,000 to the family. We say that we will limit poverty of the deserving people. One third of the average wealth to the family, or $5,000, is a fair limit to the depths we will allow any one man's family to fall. None too poor, none too rich.

2. To limit fortunes:

The wealth of this land is tied up in a few hands. It makes no difference how many years the laborer has worked, nor does it make any difference how many dreary rows the farmer has plowed, the wealth he has created is in the hands of manipulators. They have not worked any more than many other people who have nothing. Now we do not propose to hurt these very rich persons. We simply say that when they reach the place of millionaires they have everything they can use and they ought to let somebody else have something. As it is, 0.1 of 1 percent of the bank depositors own nearly half of the money in the banks, leaving 99.9 of bank depositors owning the balance. Then two thirds of the people do not even have a bank account. The lowest estimate is that 4 percent of the people own 85 percent of our wealth. The people cannot ever come to light unless we share our wealth, hence the society to do it.

3. Old-age pensions:

Everyone has begun to realize something must be done for our old people who work out their lives, feed and clothe children and are left penniless in their declining years. They should be made to look forward to their mature years for comfort rather than fear. We propose that, at the age of 60, every person should begin to draw a pension from our Government of $30 per month, unless the person of 60 or over has an income of over $1,000 per year or is worth $10,000, which is two thirds of the average wealth in America, even figured on a basis of it being frozen into a few hands. Such a pension would retire from labor those persons who keep the rising generations from finding employment.

4. To limit the hours of work:

This applies to all industry. The longer hours the human family can rest from work, the more it can consume. It makes no difference how many labor-saving devices we may invent, just as long as we keep cutting down the hours and sharing what those machines produce, the better we become. Machines can never produce too much if everybody is allowed his share, and if it ever got to the point that the human family could work only 15 hours per week and still produce enough for everybody, then praised be the name of the Lord. Heaven would be coming nearer to earth. All of us could return to school a few months every year to learn some things they have found out since we were there: All could be gentlemen: Every man a king.

5. To balance agricultural production with consumption:

About the easiest of all things to do when financial masters and market manipulators step aside and let work the law of the Lord. When we have a supply of anything that is more than we can use for a year or two, just stop planting that particular crop for a year either in all the country or in a part of it. Let the Government take over and store the surplus for the next year. If there is not something else for the farmers to plant or some other work for them to do to live on for the year when the crop is banned, then let that be the year for the public works to be done in the section where the farmers need work. There is plenty of it to do and taxes of the big fortunes at the top will supply plenty of money without hurting anybody. In time we would have the people not struggling to raise so much when all were well fed and clothed. Distribution of wealth almost solves the whole problem without further trouble.

6. To care for the veterans of our wars:

A restoration of all rights taken from them by recent laws and further, a complete care of any disabled veteran for any ailment, who has no means of support.

7. Taxation:

Taxation is to be levied first at the top for the Government's support and expenses. Swollen fortunes should be reduced principally through taxation. The Government should be run through revenues it derives after allowing persons to become well above millionaires and no more. In this manner the fortunes will be kept down to reasonable size and at the same time all the works of the Government kept on a sound basis, without debts.

Things cannot continue as they now are. America must take one of three choices, viz:

1. A monarchy ruled by financial masters—a modern feudalism.
2. Communism.
3. Sharing of the wealth and income of the land among all the people by limiting the hours of toil and limiting the size of fortunes.

The Lord prescribed the last form. It would preserve all our gains, share them among our population, guarantee a greater country and a happy people.

The need for such share-our-wealth society is to spread the truth among the people and to convey their sentiment to their Members of Congress.

Whenever such a local society has been organized, please send me notice of the same, so that I may send statistics and data which such local society can give out in their community, either through word of mouth in meetings, by circulars, or, when possible, in local newspapers.

Please understand that the Wall Street controlled public press will give you as little mention as possible and will condemn and ridicule your efforts. Such makes necessary the organizations to share the wealth of this land among the people, which the financial masters are determined they will not allow to be done. Where possible, I hope those organizing a society in one community will get in touch with their friends in other communities and get them to organize societies in them. Anyone can have copies of this article reprinted in circular form to distribute wherever they may desire, or, if they want me to have them printed for them, I can do so and mail them to any address for 60 cents per hundred or $4 per thousand copies.

I introduced in Congress and supported other measures to bring about the sharing of our wealth when I first reached the United States Senate in January 1932. The main efforts to that effect polled about six votes in the Senate at first. Last spring my plan polled the votes of nearly twenty United States Senators, becoming dangerous in proportions to the financial lords. Since then I have been abused in the newspapers and over the radio for everything under the sun. Now that I am pressing this program, the lies and abuse in the big newspapers and over the radio are a matter of daily occurrence. It will all become greater with this effort. Expect that. Meantime go ahead with the work to organize a share-our-wealth society.

Sincerely,

Huey P. Long,
United States Senator.

To: Huey P. Long,
    United States Senator, Washington, D.C.:

This is to inform you that a share-our-wealth society has been organized here with ———— members. Address and officers are as follows:

Post office _ _ _ _ _ _ _ _ _ _ _ _ _ _ _ State _ _ _ _ _ _ _ _ _

    Street address _

       President _

       Secretary _

I will go to people who know me and who personally know of the work I have done for the money that it will take for the expenses I will have to bear in this work, because, if any such thing as dues were collected from members for such expenses, the thieves of Wall Street and their newspapers and radio liars would immediately say that I had a scheme to get money.

Huey P. Long.

Every Man a King

THE CONGRESSIONAL RECORD
March 1, 1934

MR. OVERTON.* Mr. President, I ask unanimous consent to have printed in the RECORD an address by Senator HUEY P. LONG, of Louisiana, over the National Broadcasting System, on February 23, 1934, on the subject Every Man a King.

There being no objection, the address was ordered to be printed in the RECORD, as follows:

Is that a right of life, when the young children of this country are being reared into a sphere which is more owned by twelve men than it is by 120 million people?

Ladies and gentlemen, I have only thirty minutes in which to speak to you this evening, and I, therefore, will not be able to discuss in detail so much as I can write when I have all of the time and space that is allowed me for the subjects, but I will undertake to sketch them very briefly without manuscript or preparation, so that you can understand them so well as I can tell them to you tonight.

I contend, my friends, that we have no difficult problem to solve in America, and that is the view of nearly everyone with whom I have discussed the matter here in Washington and elsewhere throughout the United States—that we have no very difficult problem to solve.

It is not the difficulty of the problem which we have; it is the fact that the rich people of this country—and by rich people I mean the superrich—will not allow us to solve the problems, or rather the one little problem that is afflicting this country, because in order to

*John H. Overton, Democratic Senator from Louisiana, Long's junior colleague and ally.

cure all of our woes it is necessary to scale down the big fortunes, that we may scatter the wealth to be shared by all of the people.

We have a marvelous love for this Government of ours; in fact, it is almost a religion, and it is well that it should be, because we have a splendid form of government and we have a splendid set of laws. We have everything here that we need, except that we have neglected the fundamentals upon which the American Government was principally predicated.

How many of you remember the first thing that the Declaration of Independence said? It said, "We hold these truths to be self-evident, that there are certain inalienable rights for the people, and among them are life, liberty, and the pursuit of happiness"; and it said, further, "We hold the view that all men are created equal."

Now, what did they mean by that? Did they mean, my friends, to say that all men were created equal and that that meant that any one man was born to inherit $10 billion and that another child was to be born to inherit nothing?

Did that mean, my friends, that someone would come into this world without having had an opportunity, of course, to have hit one lick of work, should be born with more than it and all of its children and children's children could ever dispose of, but that another one would have to be born into a life of starvation?

That was not the meaning of the Declaration of Independence when it said that all men are created equal or "That we hold that all men are created equal."

Nor was it the meaning of the Declaration of Independence when it said that they held that there were certain rights that were inalienable—the right of life, liberty, and the pursuit of happiness.

Is that right of life, my friends, when the young children of this country are being reared into a sphere which is more owned by 12 men than it is by 120 million people?

Is that, my friends, giving them a fair shake of the dice or anything like the inalienable right of life, liberty, and the pursuit of happiness, or anything resembling the fact that all people are created equal; when we have today in America thousands and hundreds of thousands and millions of children on the verge of starvation in a land that is overflowing with too much to eat and too much to wear?

I do not think you will contend that, and I do not think for a moment that they will contend it.

Now let us see if we cannot return this Government to the Declaration of Independence and see if we are going to do anything regarding it. Why should we hesitate or why should we quibble or why should we quarrel with one another to find out what the difficulty is, when we know what the Lord told us what the difficulty is, and Moses wrote it out so a blind man could see it, then Jesus told us all about it, and it was later written in the Book of James, where everyone could read it?

I refer to the Scriptures, now, my friends, and give you what it says not for the purpose of convincing you of the wisdom of myself, not for the purpose, ladies and gentlemen, of convincing you of the fact that I am quoting the Scripture means that I am to be more believed than someone else; but I quote you the Scripture, or rather refer you to the Scripture, because whatever you see there you may rely upon will never be disproved so long as you or your children or anyone may live; and you may further depend upon the fact that not one historical fact that the Bible has ever contained has ever yet been disproved by any scientific discovery or by reason of anything that has been disclosed to man through his own individual mind or through the wisdom of the Lord which the Lord has allowed him to have.

But the Scripture says, ladies and gentlemen, that no country can survive, or for a country to survive it is necessary that we keep the wealth scattered among the people, that nothing should be held permanently by any one person, and that fifty years seems to be the year of jubilee in which all property would be scattered about and returned to the sources from which it originally came, and every seventh year debt should be remitted.

Those two things the Almighty said to be necessary—I should say He knew to be necessary, or else He would not have so prescribed that the property would be kept among the general run of the people, and that everyone would continue to share in it; so that no one man would get half of it and hand it down to a son, who takes half of what was left, and that son hand it down to another one, who would take half of what was left, until, like a snowball going downhill, all of the snow was off of the ground except what the snowball had.

I believe that was the judgment and the view and the law of the Lord, that we would have to distribute wealth ever so often, in order that there could not be people starving to death in a land of plenty, as there is in America today.

We have in America today more wealth, more goods, more food, more clothing, more houses than we have ever had. We have everything in abundance here.

We have the farm problem, my friends, because we have too much cotton, because we have too much wheat, and have too much corn, and too much potatoes.

We have a home-loan problem because we have too many houses, and yet nobody can buy them and live in them.

We have trouble, my friends, in the country, because we have too much money owing, the greatest indebtedness that has ever been given to civilization, where it has been shown that we are incapable of distributing the actual things that are here, because the people have not money enough to supply themselves with them, and because the greed of a few men is such that they think it is necessary that they own everything, and their pleasure consists in the starvation of the masses, and in their possessing things they cannot use, and their children cannot use, but who bask in the splendor of sunlight and wealth, casting darkness and despair and impressing it on everyone else.

"So, therefore", said the Lord, in effect, "if you see these things that now have occurred and exist in this and other countries, there must be a constant scattering of wealth in any country if this country is to survive."

"Then", said the Lord, in effect, "every seventh year there shall be a remission of debts; there will be no debts after seven years." That was the law.

Now, let us take America today. We have in America today, ladies and gentlemen, $272,000,000,000 of debt. Two hundred and seventy-two thousand millions of dollars of debts are owed by the various people of this country today. Why, my friends, that cannot be paid. It is not possible for that kind of debt to be paid.

The entire currency of the United States is only $6 billion. That is all of the money that we have got in America today. All the actual money you have got in all of your banks, all that you have got in the Government Treasury, is $6 billion; and if you took all that money and paid it out today you would still owe $266 billion; and if you took all that money and paid again you would still owe $260 billion; and if you took it, my friends, twenty times and paid it you would still owe $150 billion.

You would have to have forty-five times the entire money supply of the United States today to pay the debts of the people of America and then they would just have to start out from scratch, without a dime to go on with.

So, my friends, it is impossible to pay all of these debts, and you might as well find out that it cannot be done. The United States Supreme Court has definitely found out that it could not be done, because, in a Minnesota case, it held that when a State has postponed the evil day of collecting a debt it was a valid and constitutional exercise of legislative power.

Now, ladies and gentlemen, if I may proceed to give you some other words that I think you can understand—I am not going to belabor you by quoting tonight—I am going to tell you what the wise men of all ages and all times, down even to the present day, have all said: That you must keep the wealth of the country scattered, and you must limit the amount that any one man can own. You cannot let any man own $300 billion or $400 billion. If you do, one man can own all of the wealth that the United States has in it.

Now, my friends, if you were off on an island where there were 100 lunches, you could not let one man eat up the hundred lunches, or take the hundred lunches and not let anybody else eat any of them. If you did, there would not be anything else for the balance of the people to consume.

So, we have in America today, my friends, a condition by which about 10 men dominate the means of activity in at least 85 percent of the activities that you own. They either own directly everything or they have got some kind of mortgage on it, with a very small percentage to be excepted. They own the banks, they own the steel mills, they own the railroads, they own the bonds, they own the mortgages, they own the stores, and they have chained the country from one end to the other until there is not any kind of business that a small, independent man could go into today and make a living, and there is not any kind of business that an independent man can go into and make any money to buy an automobile with; and they have finally and gradually and steadily eliminated everybody from the fields in which there is a living to be made, and still they have got little enough sense to think they ought to be able to get more business out of it anyway.

If you reduce a man to the point where he is starving to death and bleeding and dying, how do you expect that man to get hold of any money to spend with you? It is not possible.

Then, ladies and gentlemen, how do you expect people to live, when the wherewith cannot be had by the people?

In the beginning I quoted from the Scriptures. I hope you will understand that I am not quoting Scripture to you to convince you of my goodness personally, because that is a thing between me and my Maker, that is something as to how I stand with my Maker and as to how you stand with your Maker. That is not concerned with this issue, except and unless there are those of you who would be so good as to pray for the souls of some of us. But the Lord gave his law, and in the Book of James they said so, that the rich should weep and howl for the miseries that had come upon them; and, therefore, it was written that when the rich hold goods they could not use and could not consume, you will inflict punishment on them, and nothing but days of woe ahead of them.

Then we have heard of the great Greek philosopher, Socrates, and the greater Greek philosopher, Plato, and we have read the dialog between Plato and Socrates, in which one said that great riches brought on great poverty, and would be destructive of a country. Read what they said. Read what Plato said; that you must not let any one man be too poor, and you must not let any one man be too rich; that the same mill that grinds out the extra rich is the mill that will grind out the extra poor, because, in order that the extra rich can become so affluent, they must necessarily take more of what ordinarily would belong to the average man.

It is a very simple process of mathematics that you do not have to study, and that no one is going to discuss with you.

So that was the view of Socrates and Plato. That was the view of the English statesmen. That was the view of American statesmen. That was the view of American statesmen like Daniel Webster, Thomas Jefferson, Abraham Lincoln, William Jennings Bryan, and Theodore Roosevelt, and even as late as Herbert Hoover and Franklin D. Roosevelt.

Both of these men, Mr. Hoover and Mr. Roosevelt, came out and said there had to be a decentralization of wealth, but neither one of them did anything about it. But, nevertheless, they recognized the principle. The fact that neither one of them ever did anything about it is their own problem that I am not undertaking to criticize; but had Mr. Hoover carried out what he says ought to be done, he would be retiring from the President's office, very probably, three years from now, instead of one year ago; and had

Mr. Roosevelt proceeded along the lines that he stated were necessary for the decentralization of wealth, he would have gone, my friends, a long way already, and within a few months he would have probably reached a solution of all of the problems that afflict this country today.

But I wish to warn you now that nothing that has been done up to this date has taken one dime away from these big-fortune holders; they own just as much as they did, and probably a little bit more; they hold just as many of the debts of the common people as they ever held, and probably a little bit more; and unless we, my friends, are going to give the people of this country a fair shake of the dice, by which they will all get something out of the funds of this land, there is not a chance on the topside of this God's eternal earth by which we can rescue this country and rescue the people of this country.

It is necessary to save the Government of the country, but is much more necessary to save the people of America. We love this country. We love this Government. It is a religion, I say. It is a kind of religion people have read of when women, in the name of religion, would take their infant babes and throw them into the burning flame, where they would be instantly devoured by the all-consuming fire, in days gone by; and there probably are some people of the world even today, who, in the name of religion, throw their own babes to destruction; but in the name of our good Government people today are seeing their own children hungry, tired, half-naked, lifting their tear-dimmed eyes into the sad faces of their fathers and mothers, who cannot give them food and clothing they both needed, and which is necessary to sustain them, and that goes on day after day, and night after night, when day gets into darkness and blackness, knowing those children would arise in the morning without being fed, and probably go to bed at night without being fed.

Yet in the name of our Government, and all alone, those people undertake and strive as hard as they can to keep a good government alive, and how long they can stand that no one knows. If I were in their place tonight, the place where millions are, I hope that I would have what I might say—I cannot give you the word to express the kind of fortitude they have; that is the word—I hope that I might have the fortitude to praise and honor my Government that had allowed me here in this land, where there is too much to eat and too much to wear, to starve in order that a handful of men can have so much more than they can ever eat or they can ever wear.

Now, we have organized a society, and we call it share-our-wealth society, a society with the motto "Every man a king."

Every man a king, so there would be no such thing as a man or woman who did not have the necessities of life, who would not be dependent upon the whims and caprices and ipsi dixit of the financial martyrs for a living. What do we propose by this society? We propose to limit the wealth of big men in the country. There is an average of $15,000 in wealth to every family in America. That is right here today.

We do not propose to divide it up equally. We do not propose a division of wealth, but we propose to limit poverty that we will allow to be inflicted upon any man's family. We will not say we are going to try to guarantee any equality, or $15,000 to families. No; but we do say that one third of the average is low enough for any one family to hold, that there should be a guaranty of a family wealth of around $5,000; enough for a home, an automobile, a radio, and the ordinary conveniences, and the opportunity to educate their children; a fair share of the income of this land thereafter to that family so there will be no such thing as merely the select to have those things, and so there will be no such thing as a family living in poverty and distress.

We have to limit fortunes. Our present plan is that we will allow no one man to own more than $50 million. We think that with that limit we will be able to carry out the balance of the program. It may be necessary that we limit it to less than $50 million. It may be necessary, in working out of the plans, that no man's fortune would be more than $10 million or $15 million. But be that as it may, it will still be more than any one man, or any one man and his children and their children, will be able to spend in their lifetimes; and it is not necessary or reasonable to have wealth piled up beyond that point where we cannot prevent poverty among the masses.

Another thing we propose is [an] old-age pension of $30 a month for everyone that is 60 years old. Now, we do not give this pension to a man making $1,000 a year, and we do not give it to him if he has $10,000 in property, but outside of that we do.

We will limit hours of work. There is not any necessity of having overproduction. I think all you have got to do, ladies and gentlemen, is just limit the hours of work to such an extent as people will work only so long as is necessary to produce enough for all of the people to have what they need. Why, ladies and gentlemen, let us say that all of these labor-saving devices reduce hours down to where you do not have to work but four hours a day; that is enough for these people, and then praise be the name of the Lord, if it gets that good. Let it be good and not a curse, and then we will have 5 hours a day and five days a week, or even less than that, and we might give a man a whole month off during a year, or give him two months; and we might do what other countries have seen fit to do, and what I did in Louisiana, by having schools by which adults could go back and learn the things that have been discovered since they went to school.

We will not have any trouble taking care of the agricultural situation. All you have to do is balance your production with your consumption. You simply have to abandon a particular crop that you have too much of, and all you have to do is store the surplus for the next year, and the Government will take it over. When you have good crops in the area in which the crops that have been planted are sufficient for another year, put in your public works in the particular year when you do not need to raise any more, and by that means you get everybody employed. When the Government has enough of any particular crop to take care of all of the people, that will be all that is necessary; and in order to do all of this, our taxation is going to be to take the billion-dollar fortunes and strip them down to frying size, not to exceed $50 million and if it is necessary to come to $10 million, we will come to $10 million. We have worked the proposition out to guarantee a limit upon property (and no man will own less than one third the average), and guarantee a reduction of fortunes and a reduction of hours to spread wealth throughout this country. We would care for the old people above 60 and take them away from this thriving industry and give them a chance to enjoy the necessities and live in ease, and thereby lift from the market the labor which would probably create a surplus of commodities.

Those are the things we propose to do. "Every man a king." Every man to eat when there is something to eat; all to wear something when there is something to wear. That makes us all a sovereign.

You cannot solve these things through these various and sundry alphabetical codes. You can have the NRA and PWA and CWA and the UUG and GIN and any other kind of "dadgummed" lettered code. You can wait until doomsday and see twenty-five more alphabets, but that is not going to solve this proposition. Why hide? Why quibble? You know what the trouble is. The man that says he does not know what the trouble is is just hiding his face to keep from seeing the sunlight.

God told you what the trouble was. The philosophers told you what the trouble was; and when you have a country where one man owns more than 100,000 people, or a million people, and when you have a country where there are four men, as in America, that have got more control over things than all the 130 million people together, you know what the trouble is.

We had these great incomes in this country; but the farmer, who plowed from sunup to sundown, who labored here from sunup to sundown for six days a week, wound up at the end of the time with practically nothing.

And we ought to take care of the veterans of the wars in this program. That is a small matter. Suppose it does cost a billion dollars a year—that means that the money will be scattered throughout this country. We ought to pay them a bonus. We can do it. We ought to take care of every single one of the sick and disabled veterans. I do not care whether a man got sick on the battlefield or did not; every man that wore the uniform of this country is entitled to be taken care of, and there is money enough to do it; and we need to spread the wealth of the country, which you did not do in what you call the NRA.

If the NRA has done any good, I can put it all in my eye without having it hurt. All I can see that the NRA has done is to put the little man out of business—the little merchant in his store, the little Dago that is running a fruit stand, or the Greek shoe-shining stand, who has to take hold of a code of 275 pages and study it with a spirit level and compass and looking-glass; he has to hire a Philadelphia lawyer to tell him what is in the code; and by the time he learns what the code is, he is in jail or out of business; and they have got a chain code system that has already put him out of business. The NRA is not worth anything, and I said so when they put it through.

Now, my friends, we have got to hit the root with the ax. Centralized power in the hands of a few, with centralized credit in the hands of a few, is the trouble.

Get together in your community tonight or tomorrow and organize one of our share-our-wealth societies. If you do not understand it, write me and let me send you the platform; let me give you the proof of it.

This is Huey P. Long talking, United States Senator, Washington, D.C. Write me and let me send you the data on this proposition. Enroll with us. Let us make known to the people what we are going to do. I will send you a button, if I have got enough of them left. We have got a little button that some of our friends designed, with our message around the rim of the button, and in the center "Every man a king." Many thousands of them are meeting through the United States, and every day we are getting hundreds and hundreds of letters. Share-our-wealth societies are now being organized, and people have it within their power to relieve themselves from this terrible situation.

Look at what the Mayo brothers* announced this week, these greatest scientists of all the world today, who are entitled to have more money than all the Morgans and the Rockefellers, or anyone else, and yet the Mayos turn back their big fortunes to be used for treating the sick, and said they did not want to lay up fortunes in this earth, but wanted to turn them back where they would do some good; but the other big capitalists are not willing to do that, are not willing to do what these men, 10 times more worthy, have already done, and it is going to take a law to require them to do it.

Organize your share-our-wealth society and get your people to meet with you, and make known your wishes to your Senators and Representatives in Congress.

Now, my friends, I am going to stop. I thank you for this opportunity to talk to you. I am having to talk under the auspices and by the grace and permission of the National Broadcasting System tonight, and they are letting me talk free. If I had the money, and I wish I had the money, I would like to talk to you more often on this line, but I have not got it, and I cannot expect these people to give it to me free except on some rare instance. But, my friends, I hope to have the opportunity to talk with you, and I am writing to you, and I hope that you will get up and help in the work, because

*Founders of the noted Mayo Clinic in Rochester, Minnesota.

the resolutions and bills are before Congress, and we hope to have your help in getting together and organizing your share-our-wealth society.

Now, that I have but a minute left, I want to say that I suppose my family is listening in on the radio in New Orleans, and I will say to my wife and three children that I am entirely well and hope to be home before many more days, and I hope they have listened to my speech tonight, and I wish them and all of their neighbors and friends everything good that may be had.

I thank you, my friends, for your kind attention, and I hope you will enroll with us, take care of your own work in the work of this Government, and share or help in our share-our-wealth society.

I thank you.

Redistribution of Wealth

THE CONGRESSIONAL RECORD
January 14, 1935

MR. LONG. Mr. President, I send to the desk a radio address and a letter by myself which I ask to have inserted in the RECORD.

There being no objection, the address and the letter were ordered to be printed in the RECORD, as follows:

Ladies and gentlemen, there is a verse which says that the

"Saddest words of tongue or pen
Are these: 'It might have been.' "

I must tell you good people of our beloved United States that the saddest words I have to say are:

"I told you so!"

In January 1932 I stood on the floor of the United States Senate and told what would happen in 1933. It all came to pass.

In March 1933, a few days after Mr. Roosevelt had become President and had made a few of his moves, I said what to expect in 1934. That came to pass.

As the Congress met in the early months of 1934 and I had a chance to see the course of events for that year, I again gave my belief on what would happen by the time we met again this January 1935. I am grieved to say to you that this week I had to say on the floor of the United States Senate, "I told you so!"

How I wish tonight that I might say to you that all my fears and beliefs of last year proved untrue! But here are the facts—

1. We have 1 million more men out of work now than 1 year ago.

2. We have had to put 5 million more families on the dole than we had there a year ago.

3. The newspapers report from the Government statistics that this past year we had an increase in the money made by the big men, but a decrease in the money made by the people of average and small means. In other words, still "the rich getting richer and the poor getting poorer."

4. The United States Government's Federal Deposit Insurance Corporation reports that it has investigated to see who owns the money in the banks, and they wind up by showing that two-thirds of 1 percent of the people own 67 percent of all the money in the banks, showing again that the average man and the poor man have less than ever of what we have left in this country and that the big man has more of it.

So, without going into more figures, the situation finally presents to us once more the fact that a million more people are out of work: 5 million more are on the dole, and that many more are crying to get on it; the rich earn more, the common people earn less; more and more the rich get hold of what there is in the country, and, in general, America travels on toward its route to—.

Now, what is there to comfort us on this situation? In other words, is there a silver lining? Let's see if there is. I read the following newspaper clipping on what our President of the United States is supposed to think about it. It reads as follows:

(From the New Orleans Morning Tribune, *Dec. 18, 1934)*

PRESIDENT FORBIDS MORE TAXES ON RICH—TELLS CONGRESSMEN
INCREASES MIGHT MAKE BUSINESS STAMPEDE
By the United Press

WASHINGTON, December 17.—The administration is determined to prevent any considerable increase in taxes on the very rich, many of whom pay no taxes at all, on the ground that such a plan would cause another "stampede" by business. Word has been sent up to Democratic congressional leaders that it is essential nothing be done to injure confidence. The less said about distribution of wealth, limitation of earned income, and taxes on capital, "new dealers" feel, the better.

Repeatedly since the Democrats won a two-thirds majority in both Houses in the congressional elections last month the administration has sought to assure the worker, the taxpayer, and the manufacturer that they had nothing to fear.

Meantime reports reached the Capital that fear of potential increases in inheritance taxes and gift levies at the coming Congress was in part responsible for the failure of private capital to take up a greater share of the recovery burden.

That ends the news article on what President Roosevelt has had to say.

President Roosevelt was elected on November 8, 1932. People look upon an elected President as the President. This is January 1935. We are in our third year of the Roosevelt depression, with the conditions growing worse. That says nothing about the state of our national finances. I do not even bring that in for important mention, except to give the figures:

Our national debt of today has risen to $28.5 billion. When the World War ended we shuddered in our boots because the national debt had climbed to $26 billion. But we consoled ourselves by saying that the foreign countries owed us $11 billion and that in reality the United States national debt was only $15 billion. But say that it was all of the $26 billion today. Without a war our national debt under Mr. Roosevelt has climbed up to $28.5 billion, or more than we owed when the World War ended by 2½ billions of dollars. And in the Budget message of the President he admits that next year the public debt of the United States will go up to $34 billion, or 5½ billion dollars more than we now owe.

Now this big debt would not be so bad if we had something to show for it. If we had ended this depression once and for all we could say that it is worth it all, but at the end of this rainbow of the greatest national debt in all history that must get bigger and bigger, what do we find?

One million more unemployed; 5 million more families on the dole, and another 5 million trying to get there; the fortunes of the rich becoming bigger and the fortunes of the average and little men getting less and less; the money in the banks nearly all owned by a mere handful of people, and the President of the United States quoted as saying: "Don't touch the rich!"

I begged, I pleaded, and did everything else under the sun for over 2 years to try to get Mr. Roosevelt to keep his word that he gave to us; I hoped against hope that sooner or later he would see the light and come back to his promises on which he was made President. I warned what would happen last year and for this year if he did not keep these promises made to the people.

But going into this third year of Roosevelt's administration, I can hope for nothing further from the Roosevelt policies. And I call back to mind that whatever we have been able to do to try to hold the situation together during the past three years has been forced down the throat of the national administration. I held the floor in the Senate for days until they allowed the bank laws to be amended that permitted the banks in the small cities and towns to reopen. The bank deposit guaranty law and the Frazier-Lemke farm debt moratorium law* had to be passed in spite of the Roosevelt administration. I helped to pass them both.

All the time we have pointed to the rising cloud of debt, the increases in unemployment, the gradual slipping away of what money the middle man and the poor man have into the hands of the big masters, all the time we have prayed and shouted, begged and pleaded, and now we hear the message once again from Roosevelt that he cannot touch the big fortunes.

Hope for more through Roosevelt? He has promised and promised, smiled and bowed; he has read fine speeches and told anyone in need to get in touch with him. What has it meant?

We must now become awakened! We must know the truth and speak the truth. There is no use to wait 3 more years. It is not Roosevelt or ruin; it is Roosevelt's ruin.

Now, my friends, it makes no difference who is President or who is Senator. America is for 125 million people and the unborn to come. We ran Mr. Roosevelt for the Presidency of the United States because he promised to us by word of mouth and in writing:

1. That the size of the big man's fortune would be reduced so as to give the masses at the bottom enough to wipe out all poverty; and

2. That the hours of labor would be so reduced that all would share in the work to be done and in consuming the abundance mankind produced.

*The Frazier-Lemke Act, sponsored by Senator Lynn Frazier and Representative William Lemke, both North Dakota Republicans, provided that farmers could save their farms by declaring bankruptcy, having their farms appraised by Federal officials, and paying the appraised sums to their creditors in installments over a period of five years.

Hundreds of words were used by Mr. Roosevelt to make these promises to the people, but they were made over and over again. He reiterated these pledges even after he took his oath as President. Summed up, what these promises meant was: "Share our wealth."

When I saw him spending all his time of ease and recreation with the business partners of Mr. John D. Rockefeller, Jr., with such men as the Astors, etc., maybe I ought to have had better sense than to have believed he would ever break down their big fortunes to give enough to the masses to end poverty—maybe some will think me weak for ever believing it all, but millions of other people were fooled the same as myself. I was like a drowning man grabbing at a straw, I guess. The face and eyes, the hungry forms of mothers and children, the aching hearts of students denied education were before our eyes, and when Roosevelt promised, we jumped for that ray of hope.

So therefore I call upon the men and women of America to immediately join in our work and movement to share our wealth.

There are thousands of share-our-wealth societies organized in the United States now. We want a hundred thousand such societies formed for every nook and corner of this country—societies that will meet, talk, and work, all for the purpose that the great wealth and abundance of this great land that belongs to us may be shared and enjoyed by all of us.

We have nothing more for which we should ask the Lord. He has allowed this land to have too much of everything that humanity needs.

So in this land of God's abundance we propose laws, viz:

1. The fortunes of the multimillionaires and billionaires shall be reduced so that no one person shall own more than a few million dollars to the person. We would do this by a capital levy tax. On the first million that a man was worth we would not impose any tax. We would say, "All right for your first million dollars, but after you get that rich you will have to start helping the balance of us." So we would not levy any capital levy tax on the first million one owned. But on the second million a man owns we would tax that 1 percent, so that every year the man owned the second million dollars he would be taxed $10,000. On the third million we would impose a tax of 2 percent. On the fourth million we would impose a tax of 4 percent. On the fifth million we would impose a tax of 8 percent. On the sixth million we would impose a tax of 16

percent. On the seventh million we would impose a tax of 32 percent. On the eighth million we would impose a tax of 64 percent; and on all over the eighth million we would impose a tax of 100 percent. What this would mean is that the annual tax would bring the biggest fortune down to three or four million dollars to the person because no one could pay taxes very long in the higher brackets. But $3 to 4 million is enough for any one person and his children and his children's children. We cannot allow one to have more than that because it would not leave enough for the balance to have something.

2. We propose to limit the amount any one man can earn in 1 year or inherit to $1 million to the person.

3. Now, by limiting the size of the fortunes and incomes of the big men we will throw into the Government Treasury the money and property from which we will care for the millions of people who have nothing; and with this money we will provide a home and the comforts of home, with such common conveniences as radio and automobile, for every family in America, free of debt.

4. We guarantee food and clothing and employment for everyone who should work by shortening the hours of labor to thirty hours per week, maybe less, and to eleven months per year, maybe less. We would have the hours shortened just so much as would give work to everybody to produce enough for everybody; and if we were to get them down to where they were too short, then we would lengthen them again. As long as all the people working can produce enough of automobiles, radios, homes, schools, and theaters for everyone to have that kind of comfort and convenience, then let us all have work to do and have that much of heaven on earth.

5. We would provide education at the expense of the States and the United States for every child, not only through grammar school and high school but through to a college and vocational education. We would simply extend the Louisiana plan to apply to colleges and all people. Yes; we would have to build thousands of more colleges and employ a hundred thousand more teachers; but we have materials, men, and women who are ready and available for the work. Why have the right to a college education depend upon whether the father or mother is so well to do as to send a boy or girl to college? We would give every child the right to education and a living at birth.

6. We would give a pension to all persons above 60 years of age in an amount sufficient to support them in comfortable circumstances, excepting those who earn $1,000 per year or who are worth $10,000.

7. Until we could straighten things out—and we can straighten things out in two months under our program—we would grant a moratorium on all debts which people owe that they cannot pay.

And now you have our program, none too big, none too little, but every man a king.

We owe debts in America today, public and private, amounting to $252 billion. That means that every child is born with a $2,000 debt tied around his neck to hold him down before he gets started. Then, on top of that, the wealth is locked in a vice owned by a few people. We propose that children shall be born in a land of opportunity, guaranteed a home, food, clothes, and the other things that make for living, including the right to education.

Our plan would injure no one. It would not stop us from having millionaires—it would increase them tenfold, because so many more people could make a million dollars if they had the chance our plan gives them. Our plan would not break up big concerns. The only difference would be that maybe 10,000 people would own a concern instead of 10 people owning it.

But my friends, unless we do share our wealth, unless we limit the size of the big man so as to give something to the little man, we can never have a happy or free people. God said so! He ordered it.

We have everything our people need. Too much of food, clothes, and houses—why not let all have their fill and lie down in the ease and comfort God has given us? Why not? Because a few own everything—the masses own nothing.

I wonder if any of you people who are listening to me were ever at a barbecue! We used to go there—sometimes a thousand people or more. If there were 1,000 people we would put enough meat and bread and everything else on the table for 1,000 people. Then everybody would be called and everyone would eat all they wanted. But suppose at one of these barbecues for 1,000 people that one man took 90 percent of the food and ran off with it and ate until he got sick and let the balance rot. Then 999 people would have only enough for 100 to eat and there would be many to starve because of the greed of just one person for something he couldn't eat himself.

Well, ladies and gentlemen, America, all the people of America, have been invited to a barbecue. God invited us all to come and eat and drink all we wanted. He smiled on our land and we grew crops of plenty to eat and wear. He showed us in the earth the iron and other things to make everything we wanted. He unfolded to us the secrets of science so that our work might be easy. God called: "Come to my feast."

Then what happened? Rockefeller, Morgan, and their crowd stepped up and took enough for 120 million people and left only enough for 5 million for all the other 125 million to eat. And so many millions must go hungry and without these good things God gave us unless we call on them to put some of it back.

I call on you to organize share-our-wealth societies. Write to me in Washington if you will help.

Let us dry the eyes of those who suffer; let us lift the hearts of the sad. There is plenty. There is more. Why should we not secure laws to do justice—laws that were promised to us—never should we have quibbled over the soldiers' bonus. We need that money circulating among our people. That is why I offered the amendment to pay it last year. I will do so again this year.

> *Why weep or slumber, America?*
> *Land of brave and true,*
> *With castles, clothing, and food for all*
> *All belongs to you.*
> *Ev'ry man a king, ev'ry man a king,*
> *For you can be a millionaire;*
> *But there's something belonging to others,*
> *There's enough for all people to share.*
> *When it's sunny June and December, too,*
> *Or in the wintertime or spring,*
> *There'll be peace without end,*
> *Ev'ry neighbor a friend,*
> *With ev'ry man a king.*

United States Senate,
Washington, D. C.

DEAR FRIEND: Two reports are repeatedly published in the newspapers and announced in programs rendered by the big interests in their radio programs. The first report is that I am a man of great means. If I could sell everything I own, which is not much, I could not pay one-half of my debts.

The other report repeatedly printed and circulated is that the speeches and literature which I send out are printed at Government expense. That statement is also false. With the exception of Government bulletins, etc., everything we sent out, including the enclosed document, must be paid for by us. We are frequently unable to pay some of our printing accounts, and, therefore, have to delay sending out articles requested of us until we can find money with which to do so. That fact can be verified by the accounts we have owed to the Government Printing Office.

We do not make any solicitation of you for any help, and are glad of the privilege to send anything we can on request absolutely free, in the hope that those who feel that our cause is just will make known to their neighbors some of the facts which we furnish.

Yours sincerely,

Huey P. Long,
United States Senator.

Our Growing Calamity

THE CONGRESSIONAL RECORD
January 23, 1935

MR. FRAZIER.* Mr. President, I ask unanimous consent to have printed in the RECORD a radio address delivered by Senator HUEY P. LONG, of Louisiana, over the network of the National Broadcasting Co., of Washington, D.C., on January 19 last.

There being no objection, the address was ordered to be printed in the RECORD, as follows:

Our Growing Calamity

Ladies and gentlemen, the only means by which any practical relief may be given to the people is in taking the money with which to give such relief from the big fortunes at the top. The common people haven't anything worth having; and when you put a tax that falls on them for the purpose of unemployment relief or for old-age pensions, or for anything else, you are giving nobody any relief, because you are taxing the same people who have nothing, on the pretense that you are going to give it back to them. And as a matter of fact, it all never does get back, but much of it would remain in the hands of these Washington bureaucrats and politicians.

Now, we have been clamoring for a number of relief measures. Among them was the old-age pension. We did not propose any unreasonably high old-age pension as some other plans have suggested, but we did propose that every person who reached the age of 60 should receive something around from $30 to $40 per month.

*Lynn Frazier, progressive Republican Senator from North Dakota.

We excluded from the list all people who owned $10,000 worth of property or who earned as much as $1,000 per year.

Now, along comes Mr. Roosevelt and says that he is for the old-age pension of $30 a month, but he says that it shall be paid by the States. And he says up until January 1, 1940, this $30 a month may be paid by the States to those who are over 70 years of age and after that time to those who are 65 years of age. Then he says that before they can get the $30 a month that the State government has got to put up one-half of the $30, and then it shall be paid only to those who are needy. And then he says that in order to get the money for the part the Federal Government is going to put up, that they will put a tax on all payrolls, so that the money would be taken from the very source and class to whom it is intended it would be paid.

What the Roosevelt pronouncement for old-age pensions means is that he would scuttle it inside and out. In other words, he will proceed to show how unreasonable, how impossible an old-age pension system can be, and how much harm can be done by trying to bring it about.

His plan contemplates that the Federal Government will contribute $125 million for old-age pensions throughout the United States. That is not a drop in the bucket. It will take $3½ billion to pay an old-age pension to all people who are 60 years of age; and unless the United States Government puts up all of the $3½ billion, you will not have any old age pension system that is worth anything.

Now, the only way you can get $3½ billion is by taxing the billionaires and multimillionaires, and nobody else, because if you tax the poor wage earner, who is barely making a living now, you will do more harm than good in trying to build up an old-age pension system. All the worthy movements that have been advocated throughout the United States are always praised by Mr. Roosevelt, who prescribes, in order to carry them into effect, a remedy that means you try to pull yourself up by your own bootstraps.

He admits that most of the people of America are impoverished because the rich people have all the money. He says they ought not allow them to have it all, but in the next breath he gives out a statement that the big rich must not be taxed very much, and that is as far as we ever get with him.

He rode into the President's office on the platform of redistributing wealth. He has done no such thing and has made no effort to do any such thing since he has been there. There is only one relief that can come to the American people that is of any value whatever, and that is to redistribute wealth by limiting the size of the big men's fortunes and guaranteeing that, beginning at the bottom, every family will have a living and the comforts of life. We can pass laws today providing for education, for old-age pensions, for unemployment insurance, for doles, public buildings, and anything else that we could think of, and still none of them would be worth anything unless we provided the money for them. And the money cannot be provided for them without these things doing twice as much harm as they do good unless that money is scraped off the big piles at the top and spread among the people at the bottom, who have nothing.

Any man with a thimbleful of sense who would be trying to help the poor people today by taxing the poor people so as to give the money back to them, ought to be bored for the hollow horn. Now, Mr. Roosevelt has better sense than that, but he is faced with a proposition. He has made the promise to the people that he will tear down these big fortunes by putting some reasonable limit on them, and he has further promised to build up the little man from the bottom. But he feels he doesn't dare keep that promise; he doesn't dare to keep that promise, and so, what is he doing? He makes every kind of move showing he is for this and for that; that he wants to appropriate a little money—so much for this and so much for that—but when you wind up, you find what he actually does is, that if there is any tax that can be levied on the poor people to give these things back to the poor people, that then he prescribes that kind of cure that never has cured or will cure.

The big interests realize Roosevelt's plan would not cost them anything, which is the same as saying it will be no relief to the poor. Here is the proof of that admission from the financial page of the *New York Times* of January 18, 1935:

> The action of the stock markets yesterday indicated that Wall Street was not alarmed by the President's message to Congress on social-security legislation. The financial community had been hopeful that the plan would not be so ambitious as to retard recovery. By its freedom from liquidation, when the message appeared on the news tickers, the market indicated that Wall

Street did not feel that the plan would increase taxation unduly, since it would be largely self-sustaining.

What Wall Street is saying by this dispatch is that the big men of Wall Street were a little bit apprehensive for fear Roosevelt would provide some relief or social legislation that would cost them something, but they are glad to see whatever he does will be self-sustaining. That is, the poor people who get relief will pay for it. In other words, the poor people will be allowed to help the poor people, a poor wage earner will be allowed to help his aged father or mother and take away a little more from his wife and children. "Ain't" that grand? Yet Wall Street says they are much pleased with it because it means they will not be touched for the necessary money to cure the ills of our people.

Now, our conditions today are much more deplorable than they were in [Herbert] Hoover's depression. The Roosevelt depression is just a double dose of the Hoover depression. In 1929 we started out with the public debt under Hoover of $16,931,000,000, and we wound up under Hoover with his depression showing a public debt of $19,487,000,000, or an increase of $2½ billion practically all of which increase under Hoover, however, was covered by loans made by the Reconstruction Finance Corporation, for which it had adequate security and collateral, and so, in fact, there was scarcely any such thing as an increase in the public debt under Hoover as compared to Roosevelt.

So we started in, in 1933, with the Roosevelt depression, starting from the Hoover national debt figure of $19,487,000,000. Now, when we got to December 31, 1934, the national deficit had been raised by the Roosevelt depression to $28,478,000,000, or an increase of approximately $9 billion, and most of it is just that much more debt, good and simple.

Now, how much good has been done with it? Has it cured unemployment? Get ready to laugh, if crying will do it. I will give you some unemployment figures that will shed the light as it ought to be. Here they are as they exist today:

UNEMPLOYMENT FIGURES

Half the working people in America are unemployed today. Industrial unemployment:

American Federation of Labor—1934—November__ __ 10,659,000

Farm unemployment:

Figure farm unemployment on the basis that 1929 was a normal year. That year the farm population was 30,257,000 and earned $11,941,000,000, or $394 to every farm person—that much in Hoover's first depression year. In 1933 the farm population increased by 2½ million to 32,509,000 persons who earned for the whole year $6,256,000,000 less $271,000,000 given by the Government, or the sum of $184 to the person, or 46 percent as much per farm person as under Hoover's first depression year. So the only thing that we can say is that the farm labor of 1933, as compared to the farm labor of 1929, was 54 percent unemployed so far as earnings go, and that is all that counts in unemployment figures. Figuring that 40 percent of the farm population does not work, that leaves us to figures that 19,620,000 persons are normally employed on the farm, and if we take 54 percent of them as unemployed, which they are on the basis of 1929 earnings compared to 1933 earnings, we add to the unemployed list farm laborers numbering _ _ _ _ _ _ _   10,594,800

Making the unemployed total _ _ _ _ _ _ _ _ _ _   21,253,000

Knowing that one employed person may be the breadwinner of anywhere from 1½ to 5 persons, this figure of 21,253,000 unemployed persons presents a total unemployment picture of nearly half the American people. It is about equally balanced, one-half unemployed to industry and one-half to agriculture. This does not even include the professional man as unemployed. The lawyer, doctor, accountant, architect, dentist, grocer, baker, and candlestickmaker, who cannot make a living because the people have nothing to spend with them, are not even listed as unemployed, though if the proper thing were done they would increase the list another 2,000,000 unemployed.

The figure of 10,659,000 unemployed in the industrial class would be materially increased if we included as a percentage of unemployment those working part time, some down to as low as 1 day per week.

Note also that even those who are employed earn a wage which is 43 percent below a fair standard of living. (See American Federation of Labor bulletin of January 12, 1935.)

So you see from the Government's own figures that the estimate of one-half of all our people as unemployed does not near tell the whole story.

It would be very interesting if you would just take a look to see how well the people who are employed are getting along. I have here the monthly survey of business of the American Federation of Labor dated January 12, 1935. It says this:

Comparing 1934 with 1933, according to the records, we have—

1. Average yearly wage: The worker's average yearly wage has increased 6.7 percent in these industries, while the price of food rose 11.3 percent and prices of clothing and house furnishings rose 15.3 percent. Clearly, the average employed worker's standard of living was lower in 1934 than 1933, although his average yearly income rose from $1,029 to $1,099 in 1934.

2. The average worker's income of nearly $1,099 in 1934 is below the minimum necessary to support a family of five in health and decency by $813, or 43 percent.

In other words, according to these accredited figures, those so fortunate as to be employed are living 43 percent below a reasonable standard of living at the end of the year 1934 under Roosevelt's depression.

So we sum up our condition:

We compare the Roosevelt depression with the Hoover depression and we find the Roosevelt depression debt is $9 billion more than the Hoover depression debt; the unemployment under Roosevelt has eclipsed everything Hoover ever heard about, and approximates mores than one-half the whole population of America; the wage earner of today is living further below the standard of a fair living than ever before in the history of the country; the wealth of the country is more in the hands of the big interests and the big men than it has ever been, and the common people and masses in general have less than they ever had; two-thirds of all of the money in the banks is owned by one-one hundred and fiftieth of the people, according to the figures furnished by the Government bureau itself; there are 5 million more people on the dole than

there were last year, and another 5 million people trying to get on
the dole.

We have the same promises from Mr. Roosevelt now that we
had before he was elected, with the exception he says you must not
pass any such law as will put them into effect in actual fact.

The only difference in Roosevelt before election and now is that
Roosevelt now says he is still for them, but that you must not do
anything about them. The only difference between Mr. Roosevelt
and Mr. Hoover is that things are much worse in every degree
under Mr. Roosevelt than ever under Mr. Hoover; and you could
tell what Mr. Hoover meant to do, or rather meant not to do,
whereas understanding what Mr. Roosevelt means to do com-
pared to what he does do is difficult.

There is only one way to save our people; only one way to save
America. How? Pull down wealth from the top and spread wealth
at the bottom; free people of these debts they owe; God told just
exactly how to do it all.

Many other countries have been in the shape that America is in
now; many fell and vanished like Rome and Greece, but some
cared for their people and were saved.

There was once a country in exactly the same shape as America
is today. God's prophet was there and applied the laws as God had
prescribed them. If you would just recognize that God is still alive,
that His law still lives, America would not grope today. Here is the
written record of that country that was in the same fix as America
is today. Here is what they did under the command of God's
prophet. Hear me, I read from the Bible, Nehemiah, chapter 5:

And there was a great cry of the people and of their wives
against their brethren the Jews.

For there were that said, We, our sons, and our daughters,
are many: therefore we take up corn for them, that we may eat,
and live.

Some also there were that said, We have mortgaged our
lands, vineyards, and houses, that we might buy corn, because
of the dearth.

There were also that said, We have borrowed money for the
king's tribute, and that upon our lands and vineyards.

Yet now our flesh is as the flesh of our brethren, our children
as their children; and, lo, we bring into bondage our sons and

our daughters to be servants, and some of our daughters are brought into bondage already; neither is it in our power to redeem them; for other men have our lands and vineyards.

And I was very angry when I heard their cry and these words.

Then I consulted with myself, and I rebuked the nobles, and the rulers, and said unto them, Ye exact usury, every one of his brother. And I set a great assembly against them.

And I said unto them, We after our ability have redeemed our brethren the Jews, which were sold unto the heathen; and will ye even sell your brethren? or shall they be sold unto us? Then held they their peace, and found nothing to answer.

Also, I said, it is not good that ye do; ought ye not to walk in the fear of our God because of the reproach of the heathen our enemies?

I likewise, and my brethren, and my servants, might exact of them money and corn; I pray you, let us leave off this usury.

Restore, I pray you, to them, even this day, their lands, their vineyards, their oliveyards, and their houses, also the hundredth part of the money, and of the corn, the wine, and the oil, that ye exact of them.

Then said they, We will restore them, and will require nothing of them; so will we do as thou sayest. Then I called the priests, and took an oath of them, that they should do according to this promise.

Also I shook my lap, and said, So God shake out every man from his house, and from his labor, that performeth not this promise, even thus be he shaken out, and emptied. And all the congregation said, Amen, and praised the Lord. And the people did according to this promise.

Hear me, people of America, God's laws live today. Keep them and none suffer; disregard them and we go the way of the missing. His word said that. Here is what He said:

"The profit of the earth is for all." Ecclesiastes: chapter 5, verse 9.

"And ye shall hallow the fiftieth year, and proclaim liberty throughout all the land unto all the inhabitants thereof; it shall be a jubilee unto you; and ye shall return every man unto his possession, and ye shall return every man unto his family." Leviticus: chapter 25, verse 10.

"At the end of every 7 years thou shalt make a release. * * * Every creditor that lendeth ought unto his neighbor shall release it; he shall not exact it of his * * * brother; because it is called the Lord's release." Deuteronomy: Chapter 15, verses 1 and 2.

Maybe you do not believe the Bible; maybe you do not accept God as your Supreme Lawgiver. God help you if you do not; but if you do not, then all I ask of you is to believe the simple problems of arithmetic, the tables of addition, subtraction, multiplication, and division. If you believe them, you will know that we cannot tolerate this condition of a handful of people owning nearly all and all owning nearly nothing. In a land of plenty there is no need to starve unless we allow greed to starve us to please the vanity of someone else.

I can read you what Theodore Roosevelt, Daniel Webster, Thomas Jefferson, Abraham Lincoln, Ralph Waldo Emerson, all other great Americans said. Their beliefs might be stated in the following lines of Emerson: "Give no bounties: make equal laws: secure life and prosperity and you need not give alms." Or maybe these words of Theodore Roosevelt would be proof: "We must pay equal attention to the distribution of prosperity. The only prosperity worth having is that which affects the mass of people."

It was the poet Horace who warned that Rome would fall in the days of Augustus Caesar. He expressed the line: "Penniless and great plenty."

So are our American people today. Too much to eat, to wear, or to live in; too much, and yet we are penniless and starve.

Here are the words of Pope Pius in his encyclical letter of May 18, 1932, which I, a Baptist, caused to be placed in the CONGRESSIONAL RECORD. Hear these words:

From greed arises mutual distrust that casts a blight on all human dealings; from greed arises hateful envy which makes a man consider the advantages of another as losses to himself; from greed arises narrow individualism which orders and subordinates everything to its own advantage without taking account of others, on the contrary, cruelly trampling under foot all rights of others. Hence the disorder and inequality from which arises the accumulation of the wealth of nations in the hands of a small group of individuals who manipulate the market of the world at their own caprice, to the immense harm of the masses, as we showed last year in our encyclical letter.

I call and ask you now to organize a share-our-wealth society in your community now. Don't delay. If you want to know more about it, write to me in Washington. If you want a copy of this speech, write to me for it. Help in our plan. What is it? I state it to you again:

We propose to limit the size of all big fortunes to not more than $3 to 4 million and to throw the balance in the United States Treasury; we will impose taxes every year to keep down these fortunes and to also limit the amount which any one may earn to $1 million per year, and to limit the amount any one can inherit to $1 million in a lifetime, throwing all surpluses into the United States Treasury.

Then from the immense money thus acquired we will guarantee to every family a home and the comforts of a home, including such conveniences as automobile and radio; we will guarantee education to every child and youth through college and vocational training, based upon the ability of the student and not upon the ability of the child's parents to pay the costs; we would pay flat and outright to all people over 60 years of age, a pension sufficient for their life and comfort; we would shorten the hours of work to 30 hours per week, maybe less, and to eleven months per year, maybe less; and thus share our work at living wages and to those for whom we fail to find work we would pay insurance until we do find it; we would pay the soldiers' bonus and give a sufficient supply of money to carry on our work and business.

All this can be done with ease only if we will say to the rich, "None shall be too rich!"

Won't you help in this work? Is not humanity worth the effort? How much do we need it? I will tell you.

Hear me now read you a report from our newspapers. It reads:

BABE DYING, MOTHER WALKS STREET IN HUNT FOR AID—BRAVES
BITTER COLD WHEN CHILD GROWS WORSE; FINDS NO RELIEF AT
WELFARE STATION, IS TOLD TO GO TO HOSPITAL, WALKS IN VAIN
By United Press

CHICAGO, January 16.—It was bitterly cold. Frail Mrs. Ella Martindale huddled with her four children close to an insufficient stove. The baby, 5 months old, wailed fitfully in fever under blankets on the floor.

All awaited return of Murrian Martindale, the father, who

promised when he left for his shift as a cab driver that "I'll bring something to eat, some way."

The baby's cries grew more frequent but weaker. She refused the warm water offered as a substitute for milk. Paroxysms purpled her tiny face and the older children, from 3 to 12, whimpered in sympathy and fear. Mrs. Martindale paced the floor, wrung her hands.

A strangling cough wracked the infant girl. The mother acted in desperation. Whirling blankets around the baby and a ragged coat around her own shoulders, she ordered the oldest girl to watch the other children. She raced from the room, carrying the sick child.

At an infant welfare station two blocks away she sobbed out her troubles. The women on duty were sorry, but no doctor would be present for hours. They advised her to go to St. Joseph's Hospital.

Mrs. Martindale had no car fare but she went. She walked—six blocks—with the thermometer at 16 above zero. She stumbled on the steps into the hospital.

"My baby," she sobbed to a nurse, "she's sick." The nurse peered into the blankets, then took the little bundle.

"She's dead," she said.

Good night, my friends. I thank you!

Educational Program for Share Our Wealth Society

THE CONGRESSIONAL RECORD
February 7, 1935

MR. LONG. Mr. President, I send to the desk, and, in order to save time, ask to have printed in the RECORD a statement entitled "Educational Program for Share Our Wealth Society."

There being no objection, the statement was ordered to be printed in the RECORD, as follows:

Educational Program For Share Our Wealth Society—Government Assumes the Cost and Burden To Guarantee College, Professional, and Vocational Education To All Students

Under the present policy of government the young man and young woman whose parents are possessed of means can be given a college education or vocational and professional training. There are some exceptions to this rule; that is to say, that in some few cases students can find work by which to pay their expenses through college. As a general rule, however, only those with parents possessing extraordinary means can attend college.

"All men are created equal", says the Declaration of Independence, and to all those born the Constitution of our Nation guarantees "life, liberty, and the pursuit of happiness."

These provisions of our immortal national documents are not observed when the right to education rests upon the financial ability of one's parents rather than upon the mental capacity of a student to learn and his energy to apply himself to the proper study necessary for him to learn.

The share-our-wealth program contemplates that from the billions of excess revenue brought into the United States Treasury by limiting fortunes to a few million dollars to any one person, that such large sums will be expended by the Government as will afford college education and professional training to all students based upon their mental capacity and energy rather than upon the wealth of their parents. Such an education contemplates not only the scholarship but such supplies and living costs as a student may have in order to attend college.

This will transfer the youth of our land into making preparation for building a better and greater nation. It will take their surplus labor out of the ranks of employment and afford more room for others; it will mean an immediate expansion of our educational facilities and the bringing back into active service of hundreds of thousands of learned instructors whose intellect and capacities, now idle, may be used for the moral, spiritual, and intellectual uplift of the Nation. Architects, engineers, builders, material men, and craftsmen now idle would find extensive and continued field for employment in providing and maintaining such extended educational facilities in the Nation.

All in all, the program is one of national organization; it means no great or burdensome outlay because there is a surplus of the goods and things needed for the care of all students, and the consuming of the same will immediately aid our problems of overproduction.

Huey P. Long,
United States Senator.

Our Plundering Government

THE CONGRESSIONAL RECORD
March 4, 1935

MR. LONG. Mr. President, I ask unanimous consent to have printed in the RECORD a radio speech which I delivered over the National Broadcasting Co. system on Sunday, February 10, 1935.

There being no objection, the speech was ordered to be printed in the RECORD, as follows:

Ladies and gentlemen, the introduction which my friend has given me is not quite complete. I wanted it to be more or less complete—that I am still in the Democratic Party; so I am going to reintroduce myself to this audience, hoping that you will believe that I am even a better Democrat than I was here three or four years ago. In fact, I believe you already know that. I am Huey P. Long. I am now a United States Senator. I am also national Democratic committeeman from the State of Louisiana; I am also the chairman of the Louisiana State Democratic Central Committee; and I am also the head of the Louisiana Democratic majority organization, as well as being a member of the National Democratic Party councils. And I intend to make you a speech along the lines of democratic government for the few minutes that have been assigned me by the Columbia Broadcasting System.

This being a Sunday night, it would be better that I perhaps stay within the confines of the Scriptures as much as I can, so I will read from Proverbs, chapter 30, verses 7 to 9, as follows:

"Two things have I required of Thee; deny me them not before I die:

"Remove far from me vanity and lies; give me neither poverty nor riches; feed me with food convenient for me:

"Lest I be full, and deny Thee, and say, Who is the Lord? or lest I be poor, and steal, and take the name of my God in vain."

That ends the quotation from Proverbs, written by Solomon, the wisest of all men. I am not going to reread, but I want to restate for fear some may not have grasped the entire significance of that little phrase that I have read; I will restate the theory. "Give me neither riches nor poverty", says the Scriptures, "lest I be vain and say, Who is the Lord, or if I be poor, I become a thief."

The Bible takes it as axiomatic that one is as evil as the other; that is, that an extremely rich man is as evil as an extremely poor man, and the Bible takes it as axiomatic that the extremely rich man must by the nature of the thing be an evil man; and the poor man must by the nature of the thing be in the direction of a thief. Now, that is the Bible. Maybe you don't think so. Wait a minute; I will give you a little more: St. Matthew 19:23, 24:

"Then said Jesus unto His disciples, 'Verily I say unto you that a rich man shall hardly enter in to the Kingdom of Heaven.

" 'And again I say unto you it is easier for a camel to go through the eye of a needle than for a rich man to enter into the Kingdom of God.' "

Of course, many people have been trying to tell you that that Biblical commandment meant something else; they have been trying to tell you that it didn't mean a needle but some hole in the wall; but when you go back up and read Proverbs and then read St. Matthew you have quite some little difficulty in saying anything except what the Bible said it means; that is, that it is practically impossible for a rich man to enter heaven; but if you have any doubt about it, let me read you something else. I read you from the Book of James, chapter 5. That is in the New Testament:

"Go to now, ye rich men, weep and howl for your miseries that shall come upon you."

That will be found in the fifth chapter of the Book of James. Following along those lines, it says:

"Ye have lived in pleasure on the earth;

"Ye have heaped treasure together for the last days.

"Your riches are corrupted, and your garments are moth-eaten.

"Your gold and silver is cankered; and the rust of them shall be a witness against you, and shall eat your flesh as it were fire."

So, then, ladies and gentlemen, while I am not presuming to

preach you any sermon, I am only undertaking to establish (and I can cite you a hundred other quotations equally as cogent), I am only seeking to establish that extreme poverty is looked upon by the Bible as the substance to make a man a thief, and extreme riches is looked upon by the Bible to make a man just as bad. And so said Solomon, and so say the various other provisions of the Scriptures.

Riches or poverty make of a man just the exact opposite of what is intended by the Bible, and by the Lord. You will find, my friends, that God knew, and that we ought to know, that no one can have very much more than he needs without depriving someone else of what he must have to live. But if very rich people we must have, then naturally we must have very poor people. To have very rich people, we have to have very poor people. The whole thing is a seesaw; when one set of our people go high up in the air, the common people must come way down, and if the side of the seesaw on which the rich people sit is pushed up too high, the other side must carry us down in the ground. So has America's seesaw worked, that the very rich have gone so high, that the very poor are going down into their graves.

But there could be a seesaw on a near an even level, where we could go up and down, but never so low as to wreck us. That is the kind of a seesaw we want. Not exactly a level for everybody, but don't have one man so high that he must of necessity crowd another man to his grave.

God said none too rich; none too poor. For, said the Lord, the rich will defy the Lord and the poor will become a thief. "Feed all with food convenient to them."

I happened at one time to be Governor of the State of Louisiana—from 1928 to 1932. When I became Governor of that State we had 1,500 men in the penitentiary. During the depression times that I served as Governor, that 1,500 men grew to 3,000 men in the penitentiary—double the enrollment in the penitentiary in four years. Now, I don't think I had inculcated into the population that kind of a disposition, that there would be twice as many convicts in the penitentiary in those two or three years' time as prior to my time as Governor. So I undertook to look into the matter and find the reason. The days of the depression only tended to make people criminals, I found.

Now, my friends, I am going to skip just a little bit of what I had

intended to say tonight, to get to the cold facts as to what is
responsible for conditions, and the correctives which I am going to
apply. Speaking over this broadcast tonight from coast to coast I
notice I have a large number of eastern stations. I didn't know that
when I came here, so therefore, some of the manuscript which I
had prepared will be discarded, because I am particularly anxious
that I may be permitted to reach into this eastern territory and to
say some of the things I have often wanted to be heard by the
people living in the Eastern States. I am going to read you from
Theognis, one of the great Greeks. I am going to read you from
him for this reason, that I am not unmindful that many people
think the Scriptures is a worn-out book. It is not, but there are
some people who don't accept the Bible and say some men are
smarter than the Scriptures, and they particularly point to the
philosophers of ancient Greece, and among those most often referred to are such men as Socrates, Plato, and Theognis.

I suppose Plato is looked upon as being probably the greatest—
Theognis probably the next. I am going to read you from Theognis, one of the Greek philosophers, then I will read you from
Plato. Said this great Greek philosopher in these words: "Fullness
(plenty) hath ere now destroyed far more men, look you, than
famine, to wit, as many as were desirous of having more than their
share."

Also, a little later on, if you care to have me read, I will give you
what Plato said along the same lines. Here is what Plato said: "The
citizen (of this ideal republic) must indeed be happy and good, and
the legislator will seek to make him so; but very rich and very good
at the same time he cannot be."

In other words, said Plato, long before the birth of Jesus Christ,
it is impossible for a man to be very rich and very good at the same
time. Now, you may think that it is a different proposition in
America. Well, ladies and gentlemen, there never were fortunes
made in any country through as many tactics of brigandages and
through as many crimes and demeanors of men in his position as
the American fortunes. I am not going to undertake to defame
those men, but I can take you any fortune you wish to write me
about and show you it has not been amassed by any tactics other
than by force and crimes. I can take you the Morgan fortune, the
Rockefeller fortune, or the Mellon fortune, or any fortune you
wish to inquire about. The Rockefellers broke every railroad rate

and every railroad law ever put on the books before they got them. They sent more men to their graves than all of the bandits in Chicago can kill if they lived to be 1,000 years old apiece.

The Morgan fortune was started by J. P. Morgan, Jr., who was the father of the J. P. Morgan of today, selling some refused carbines to Fremont's army.* Many other things might be declared responsible for the Morgan fortune. The Bosco fiasco in South and Central America is sufficient to condemn the Mellon fortune, but just let us say they were all properly and well acquired. Leave it at that; however they were acquired you cannot get away from the Scriptures or the philosophers who say that it is impossible for a man to be very good and very rich at the same time.

Now, maybe then you don't believe the Greek philosophers, or maybe then you don't believe the Scriptures either. Then I will not ask you to believe anything very difficult; I am not going to ask you to believe fractions. I will only ask you to believe the simple tables of arithmetic—and if you will concede the principles of the four elementary problems of arithmetic—addition, subtraction, multiplication, and division, I will have no fault with you tonight, but before going into that, let me give you another succinct proof as to whether or not this country was properly founded and whether or not it is still being steered on the course it was originally intended.

I am going to read to you from the Covenant of the Pilgrims. You have talked about the Pilgrim Fathers, some of my wise critics, and you have said I am preaching a doctrine contrary to the doctrine of the Pilgrim Fathers on which the country was founded. Well, of course, you newspaper people who have written that—not all of you newspapers have written that—but you magazines who have written, and you would-be statesmen (and that is about as good as any of us ever get to be, is the class of a would-be statesman), but some of our great statesmen who said I am going so far as to say I am going counter to the Covenant of the Pilgrim Fathers—did you ever read the Covenant of the Pilgrim Fathers? I know you didn't, and I will read it to you. Here it is. I am now reading from the Bradford history presented by the New England Society in the city of New York to its members (pp. 56, 57, 58):

*John Charles Fremont, noted explorer and first Presidential candidate of the Republican Party, was a general in the Union Army during the Civil War.

"It will be meete I here inserte these conditions, which are as foloweth: (This is the old Pilgrim Contract.) Year 1620, July 1st."

Now I am going to skip to no. 7, if you don't mind:

"7. He that shall carie his wife & children, or servants, shall be alowed for everie person now aged 16. years & upward, a single share in ye division. or if he provid them necessaries, a duble share, or if they be between 10. years old and 16., then 2. of them to be reconed for a person, both in transportation and devision."

Just before that, I read you no. 6:

"6. Whosoever cometh to ye colonie hereafter, or putteth any into ye stock, shall at the ende of ye 7. years be alowed proportionably to ye time of his so doing."

Now I read you no. 5, because I am reading you in inverse order:

"5. That at ye end of ye 7. years, we capital & profits, viz. the houses, lands, goods, and chatles, be equally devided betwixte ye adventurers, and planters; wch done, every man shall be free from other of them of any debt or detriments concerning this adventure."

In other words, the Pilgrim Fathers had a contract that they would keep the word of the Lord. The Bible commanded them that at the end of seven years that they ought to remit all debts, and they ought to see that the wealth was redistributed, so none would have too much, and none would be too poor. And the Pilgrim Fathers who founded the country wrote it into the Covenant, not to do what HUEY LONG said, because I am not advocating an equal division of the wealth every seven years, but they said more than I ever said, in order that they would never have such a thing as concentration of wealth in the hands of the few, that every seven years they would divide up the wealth among all of them equally, and at the end of every seven years they would remit all debts. Now some of you wise men who have been talking about me not minding the faith of the Pilgrim Fathers, go off and read that and weep a little bit more and see what other faith is there that has been unminded by the proposition I have offered in the United States Senate.

My friends, today a young man attending Columbia University came to see me. I knew him in Louisiana, and his folks were always friends to me, and they voted for me for every office I ever ran for. He came along today and told me he could not keep up his course at college unless he could borrow $250. He wanted me to loan him $250. And I didn't have it to loan to him. And I thought how tragic it was that that young man had to go away and be turned away from Columbia University while undertaking to complete an ordinary course at college, which he had the mental capacity to absorb, while other people have the opportunity by reason of the wealthy condition of their parents, but don't have the mental capacity to do it.

So I said to this young man, "I am very sorry for you. But," I said, "before you leave I want to give you something." And I gave him the educational program of the share-our-wealth society. Let me tell you what that is. We propose, if we have the capacity to conscript soldiers and train them year after year, that we will do no conscripting, but that just the same we will train these people in other lines. We propose that education will be taken over as a function of the United States Government and that every girl and boy will be permitted to absorb an education not only through grammar school and high school but through colleges and vocational and professional training, and the living costs and school costs and other such costs will be absorbed as a matter of Government costs.

Now you say where are you going to get the money? Wait a moment. That is not all we propose. We say further we ought to guarantee through our share-our-wealth program that we will afford to every deserving family in this country, and by deserving we mean every family not in the penitentiary or insane asylum, or even those in the insane asylum for that matter—we say we will guarantee to every deserving family in this country a home and the comforts of a home, and included in such comforts would be such things as a radio and automobile, and such other conveniences and necessities of life.

We would guarantee up to not less than $5,000, or an average of one third of the average wealth in this country—to every deserving family to begin with. Then we would reduce the hours of employment to 30 hours a week, maybe less, and 11 months to the year, maybe less. We would reduce employment to such a condition that we would share the work so that people would work only so long as it became necessary to produce the things needed by the people, and that we would reduce the hours so much as would be necessary to have everybody employed, rather than to have one employed too much of the time, and some employed none of the time.

We would include in our program old-age pensions to those above 60 years of age of around $30 to $40 to the month. Also, ladies and gentlemen, we would undertake to discharge along with that, the bonus that we owe to the soldiers.

Now you want to know where are we going to get the money? We will levy a capital levy tax on all big fortunes in the United States. We will say to a millionaire: "We are not worried about your first million dollars. If you wish to be a millionaire, we will not worry about your first million dollars, and that is more than you can spend during your lifetime and your children's lifetime adequately and properly." But we will say if you wish to be a millionaire, we will not be concerned with that, but if you wish to be above a millionaire we will step in for the welfare of the country to a certain point. So we will say, keep your first million dollars. But after you have got more than one million, we charge you 1 percent on the second million, 2 percent on the third million, 4 percent on the fourth million, 8 percent on the fifth million, 16 percent on the sixth million, 32 percent on the seventh million, 64 percent on the eighth million, and 100 percent on the ninth million, which means that in time that there would be no man in this country that could own more than $2½ to $4 million. And that would be our limit upon the amount that any one man would be permitted to own in this country, and when we have done that, we will throw into the Treasury of the United States Government tomorrow $165,000,000,000. And with $100 billion we can give to every family in this country a home and the comforts of a home, and with the balance of the money we can have an improvement program which will discharge every obligation this country owes to its citizens and continually supply the entire population of America through employment and other facilities that reducing these fortunes of the big men would give the Government the means with which to do so.

Ladies and gentlemen, this is Huey P. Long talking, for the benefit of those who have just tuned in, and for the benefit of those who yet remain.

Now, let us see here. We have organized share-our-wealth societies. Maybe some of you good people here in the East who are listening to me don't believe what I am saying. You don't believe it is possible to have that much money, do you? Well, there is a big financial writer here in this country called Roger W. Babson, hired by Wall Street and the newspapers of Wall Street. Let's see what he says. Mr. Roger Babson says in 1934: "With intensive production and proper distribution, every family in the country should receive an income of $10,000 per year, with everybody from 20 to 50 years old working 8 months annually."

Now, Mr. Babson says that there is $10,000 a year in earnings. Well, now, let's reduce this financial writer's figures by two and say there is $5,000, and then let's say we will give $3,000 of that to the multimillionaires to spread among their children, and things of that kind in years to come; that would still leave an income of not below $2,000. That would be sufficient, after a man has a home and the comforts of a home, that all might live in respectability.

I am not going to read some other figures to support that, but I have them here and anybody who wants them can write and get them. Mr. Roosevelt has had two men who made this estimate. One of them estimated there would never be less than $4,370 to the family, and the other estimated there would never be less than $5,000 to the family. Take any set of figures you want, and it is two times as much as I contend to be necessary to carry the entire American population.

Why have this misery and this distress in America? Why have people hungry? Why have people naked for the want of clothes to wear? Why have our people homeless? Why have all these millions of unemployed? We have the food to feed the people. Why let it rot while people starve? We have the clothes and the cotton and wool to make more clothes and more than anyone will ever need to wear. Why have all of them fall to pieces and mold while people shiver for the lack of them? We have the houses to live in and the material and labor to build more houses to live in. Why have men, women, and children crying for a place to rest their heads, while the walls inside the houses fall to ruin for lack of human habitation?

Why? Because Mr. Franklin D. Roosevelt has refused to carry out his promise to pull down the size of the big fortunes and to use the money thus taken to end all such things as poverty among the people. With all these many extra things which we have, with this surplus of food, clothes, and houses, to let our people go to ruin for the lack of them is a shame on the birth of manhood. The United States is like a fool carrying a loaf of bread under his arm and starving to death at the same time. We propose to share our wealth.

What are we going to do about these debts? We have $252 billion of debts, public and private debts. Two hundred and fifty-two billion dollars! That is $2,000 to every man, woman, and child in the United States in debts. In the days before the war—in the old slave days in the South—a colored man could buy his freedom for $1,500 or $2,000; and yet today, ladies and gentlemen, all of the whites and all of the blacks come into this world with $2,000 of debts as their inheritance. There used to be a time when we carried a silver spoon and a cup or a baby rattle to a baby at the time of his birth. We have changed that. Today we tie a $2,000 debt around his neck, and many are never able to pay it throughout their entire lifetime.

Europe owes us $11 billion that we can't collect, and we had to excuse Europe. We gave Europe a moratorium of one year, and they take a moratorium after that; and we gave them a year and they take the balance of the time. Now, if Europe can't pay the $11 billion—and that includes England, France, Russia, Czechoslovakia, Jugoslavia, Lithuania, and every other Slovakia they have got over there—if all of them put together can't pay $11 billion, then how are 125,000,000 people ever going to pay $252 billion?

Now, if you will turn back to the law of the Lord, Deuteronomy, fifteenth chapter, the first verse, you will find where He commanded you have got to remit these debts every seventh year. Now, I have been condemned because I wrote a law in Louisiana that all persons burdened with debts which they could not pay would have the right to have these debts suspended on proper showing. They have defamed that law, but in Louisiana it has saved many a person, and I would rather have that.

Well, we have had other things to contend with. I see here is a little report from Kansas City, Mo. I read to you from the Kansas City (Mo.) Journal-Post of Monday, January 7, 1935:

[From the Kansas City (Mo.) Journal Post,
Monday, Jan. 7, 1935]

EVICTED WOMAN WISHES ROOSEVELT COULD SEE
"FULFILLMENT" OF PROMISE

Mrs. Kathleen McDonald sat on the edge of a bare bed Monday morning and watched movers, under the watchful eyes of a deputy sheriff, carry the furniture from her home at 3743 Main Street.

"President Roosevelt," she said, "told the Nation only a few months ago that no one would lose a home by foreclosure. I wish he could be here this morning to see these movers, backed by the circuit court and the sheriff, throw me out of my house."

A moving man entered the room.

"I'm sorry, lady," he said, apologetically, "but we have to have the bed now."

KICKED OUT, PENNILESS

Mrs. McDonald arose and walked to the window—stared out at the damp, foggy street scene. Her voice choked, tears streamed down her cheeks.

"Oh, God," she sobbed, "why do they have to do this to us. This home represents the life savings of myself and my sister— $20,000—and now we're being kicked out, penniless.

"This house was not only our shelter but our livelihood, for we kept roomers. Now we're losing it, and we have no place to go. We do not even know where we'll sleep. We'll have to hunt jobs and begin all over.

"I wired President Roosevelt Monday morning, but I don't suppose he'll answer. And just to think, he said that no home . would be foreclosed."

Oh, yes; my good friend Mr. Roosevelt rode in on the program that he was going to bring poverty to an absolute end. He was going to bring poverty to an absolute end! He promised to bring down these big fortunes. He promised to see there was no such thing as a man without a home and the comforts of a home. He promised there would be no such thing as an unemployed man or woman, and how many have you got unemployed today? Twenty-one million unemployed; and if you consider the fact that 54 percent of the farm labor is unemployed today, and if you will add these to the industrial statistics, you have got 21 million unemployed; and if you doubt that go over and take the statistics of the ERA—the relief organization—and you will find that today they have got 19½ million people on the relief dole today; going to show you there is probably more than 21 million unemployed. Count 2½ to 3 people to every unemployed person, since 1 man usually earns the bread for 3, and you have half of the American people today unemployed; and that does not include the doctor, the lawyer, and the candlestick maker, or the professional man, because while he may give up his office he is still hoping somebody will come along and give him a little business.

Right in my mail today I received a letter from Kansas City signed by a little girl. It reads:

Kansas City, Kans.,
January 19, 1935.

DEAR SENATOR LONG: I listened to your speech over the radio. And you quoted verses from the Bible. I also read the Bible.

I do not believe Mr. Roosevelt has a Bible. And if he did have he could not read it. I am a poor little girl 12 years old, or I would buy him one. So if you will please buy Mr. Roosevelt a small Bible and mark the chapters of Deuteronomy, the eleventh chapter to the twelfth, subject a blessing and a curse:

Fifteenth verse: "And I will send grass in thy fields for thy cattle that thou may eat and be full."

Sixteenth verse: "Take heed to yourselves that your heart be not deceived and aye turn aside and serve other gods and worship them."

Seventeenth verse: "And then the Lord's wrath be kindled against you. And He shut up the heavens that there be no rain and that the land yield not her fruit, and lest ye perish quickly from off the good land which the Lord giveth you."

I believe in God and I think God must have closed up the heavens last summer as a warning to some of the selfish ones on this earth.

Yours truly,

Dorothy McKienzie,
1204 Bunker St.

Well, Mr. Roosevelt don't have to read the Bible; all he has to do is read his own promises and keep them. If Roosevelt will keep his promises to the American people, we won't have all of this trouble.

Ladies and gentlemen, the bank deposits show two thirds of 1 percent own two thirds of 100 percent of all the money in the banks. In other words, two thirds of 1 percent own what two thirds of 100 percent ought to own. That is the disproportionate balance that maintains today in regard to the bank balances. What is the correction? The only correction is, ladies and gentlemen, that we must return to the law of the Lord: None shall be too big; none shall be too little. We should go out and start immediately so that we will have the jubilee brought back to where it was intended. Maybe not so completely as the Bible intended, but in some respects, that the fortunes of the little will not be allowed to become less, and the fortunes of the big will not be allowed to become bigger. That being done, our problems are all solved.

Why have those uneducated? Why have people in misery? Why have people homeless? In this distress, the Lord has smiled upon this land, so I invite you, I beg you, I beseech you, come into the share-our-wealth society; organize in your community a share-our-wealth society—not on socialistic lines, not on communistic lines, not on the lines of fascism, not on the lines of bolshevism, but on the lines that we will say that when a man reaches up into the millions of dollars, he has enough, and when a man who is below the average of a home for his family, that he has not had enough. That program which says we will shorten the hours and take up the slack in labor. That program which guarantees to every boy and girl the right to be educated according to their mental capacity, and not according to the financial capacity of their parents.

I hope you will join our share-our-wealth society. This is HUEY P. LONG, United States Senator, talking to you. I hope you will go into your neighborhood, and into the neighborhood next to you there, and get your friends to organize share-our-wealth societies.

If you want any information, write to me here in Washington, D. C., and I will give you any information which you may need without any charge whatever. I hope, ladies and gentlemen, that you may see fit to help in this work. I thank you.

Our Blundering Government

THE CONGRESSIONAL RECORD
March 12, 1935

MR. LONG. Mr. President, I ask to have a speech printed in the RECORD.

MR. ROBINSON. What is the request?

MR. LONG. To have a speech printed in the RECORD.

The PRESIDENT pro tempore. Is there objection to the request of the Senator from Louisiana?

MR. ROBINSON. I should like to know what the speech is.

MR. LONG. I suggest the Senator look at it and see if he objects to it. It is a speech which I made over the radio the other night.

MR. CONNALLY. Mr. President, I am not going to object, but I think the Senator should have enough respect for the Senate to indicate what it is he asks to have printed.

MR. LONG. Everyone in the Senate listened to it the other night, or read it in the New York Times. I want it to go to the remainder of the country.

MR. CONNALLY. The Senator handed in something and asked to have it printed in the RECORD, but did not state what it was.

MR. LONG. It is my last radio speech.

MR. CONNALLY. The Senate is entitled to that information.

MR. LONG. I beg the Senate's pardon.

The PRESIDENT pro tempore. Without objection, the speech will be printed in the RECORD.

There being no objection, the speech, broadcast from

Washington, D.C., March 7, 1935, was ordered to be printed in the RECORD, as follows:

Ladies and gentlemen, it has been publicly announced that the White House orders of the Roosevelt administration have declared war on HUEY LONG. The late and lamented, the pampered ex-crown prince, Gen. Hugh S. Johnson,* one of those satellites loaned by Wall Street to run the Government, and who, at the end of his control over and dismissal from the NRA, pronounced it "as dead as a dodo", this Mr. Johnson was apparently selected to make the lead-off speech in this White House charge begun last Monday night. The Johnson speech was followed by more fuss and fury on behalf of the administration by spellbinders in and out of Congress.

In a far-away island, when a queen dies, her first favorite is done the honor to be buried alive with her. The funeral procession of the NRA (another one of these new-deal schisms or isms) is about ready to occur. It is said that General Johnson's speech of Monday night to attack me was delivered on the eve of announcing the publication of his obituary in the *Red Book* Magazine. Seems then that soon this erstwhile prince of the deranged alphabet makes ready to appear at the funeral of NRA like unto the colored lady in Mississippi who there asserted: "I is de wife of dese remains."

I shall undertake to cover my main subject and make answer to these gentlemen in the course of this speech tonight.

It will serve no purpose to our distressed people for me to call my opponents more bitter names than they call me. Even were I able, I have not the time to present my side of the argument and match them in billingsgate or profanity.

What is this trouble with this administration of Mr. [Franklin D.] Roosevelt, Mr. [Hugh S.] Johnson, Mr. [James A.] Farley,† Mr. [Vincent] Astor, and all their spoilers and spellbinders? They think that HUEY LONG is the cause of all their worry. They go gunning for me. But, am I the cause of their misery? They are like

---

*General Hugh S. Johnson, originator and administrator of the Selective Service Act during World War I, and administrator of President Roosevelt's National Recovery Act.

†James A. Farley, manager of Franklin D. Roosevelt's first Presidential campaign, served simultaneously as Postmaster of the United States and Chairman of the Democratic National Committee from 1932 to 1940.

old Davy Crockett, who went out to hunt a possum. He saw in the gleam of the moonlight that a possum in the top of a tree was going from limb to limb. He shot and missed. He saw the possum again. He fired a second time and missed again. Soon he discovered that it was not a possum he saw at all in the top of that tree. It was a louse in his own eyebrow.

I do not make this illustration to do discredit to any of these gentlemen. I make it to show how often we imagine we see great trouble being done to us by someone at a distance, when, in reality, all of it may be a fault in our own make-up.

The trouble with the Roosevelt administration is that when their schemes and isms have failed, these things I told them not to do and voted not to do, that they think it will help them to light out on those of us who warned them in the beginning that the tangled messes and noble experiments would not work. The Roosevelt administration has had its way for two years. They have been allowed to set up or knock down anything and everybody. There was one difference between [Herbert] Hoover and Roosevelt. Hoover could not get the Congress to carry out the schemes he wanted to try. We managed to lick him on a roll call in the United States Senate time after time. But, different with Mr. Roosevelt. He got his plans through Congress. But on cold analysis they were found to be the same things Hoover tried to pass and failed.

The kitchen cabinet that sat in to advise Hoover was not different from the kitchen cabinet which advised Roosevelt. Many of the persons are the same. Many of those in Roosevelt's kitchen cabinet are of the same men or set of men who furnished employees to sit in the kitchen cabinet to advise Hoover.

Maybe you see a little change in the man waiting on the tables, but back in the kitchen the same set of cooks are fixing up the victuals for us that cooked up the mess under Hoover.

Why, do you think this Roosevelt's plan for plowing up cotton, corn, and wheat; and for pouring milk in the river, and for destroying and burying hogs and cattle by the millions, all while people starve and go naked—do you think those plans were the original ideas of this Roosevelt administration? If you do, you are wrong. The whole idea of that kind of thing first came from Hoover's administration. Don't you remember when Mr. Hoover proposed to plow up every fourth row of cotton? We laughed him into scorn. President Roosevelt flayed him for proposing such a thing in the speech which he made from the steps of the capitol in Topeka, Kans.

And so we beat Mr. Hoover on his plan. But when Mr. Roosevelt started on his plan, it was not to plow up every fourth row of cotton as Hoover tried to do. Roosevelt's plan was to plow up every third row of cotton, just one-twelfth more cotton to be plowed up than Hoover proposed. Roosevelt succeeded in his plan.

So it has been that while millions have starved and gone naked; so it has been that while babies have cried and died for milk; so it has been that while people have begged for meat and bread, Mr. Roosevelt's administration has sailed merrily along, plowing under and destroying the things to eat and to wear, with tear-dimmed eyes and hungry souls made to chant for this new deal so that even their starvation dole is not taken away, and meanwhile the food and clothes craved by their bodies and souls go for destruction and ruin. What is it? Is it government? Maybe so. It looks more like St. Vitus dance.

Now, since they sallied forth with General Johnson to start the war on me, let us take a look at this NRA that they opened up around here two years ago. They had parades and Fascist signs just as Hitler, and Mussolini. They started the dictatorship here to regiment business and labor much more than anyone did in Germany or Italy. The only difference was in the sign. Italy's sign of the Fascist was a black shirt. Germany's sign of the Fascist was a swastika. So in America they sidetracked the Stars and Stripes, and the sign of the Blue Eagle was used instead.

And they proceeded with the NRA. Everything from a peanut stand to a power house had to have a separate book of rules and laws to regulate what they did. If a peanut stand started to parch a sack of goobers for sale, they had to be careful to go through the rule book. One slip and he went to jail. A little fellow who pressed a pair of pants went to jail because he charged 5 cents under the price set in the rule book. So they wrote their NRA rule book, codes, laws, etc. They got up over 900 of them. One would be as thick as an unabridged dictionary and as confusing as a study of the stars. It would take 40 lawyers to tell a shoe-shine stand how to operate and be certain he didn't go to jail.

Some people came to me for advice, as a lawyer, on how to run a business. I took several days and then couldn't understand it

myself. The only thing I could tell them was that it couldn't be
much worse in jail than it was out of jail with that kind of thing
going on in the country, and so to go on and do the best they
could.

The whole thing of Mr. Roosevelt, as run under General Johnson, became such a national scandal that Roosevelt had to let
Johnson slide out as the scapegoat. Let them call for an NRA
parade tomorrow and you couldn't get enough people to form a
funeral march.

It was under this NRA and the other funny alphabetical combi-
nations which followed it that we ran the whole country into a
maresnest. The Farleys and Johnsons combed the land with
agents, inspectors, supervisors, detectives, secretaries, assistants,
etc., all armed with the power to arrest and send to jail whomever
they found not living up to some rule in one of these 900 catalogs.
One man whose case reached the Supreme Court of the United
States was turned loose because they couldn't even find the rule he
was supposed to have violated in a search throughout the United
States.

And now it is with PWA's, CWA's, NRA's, AAA's, J-UG's,
G-IN's, and every other flimsy combination that the country finds
its affairs and business tangled to where no one can recognize it.
More men are now out of work than ever; the debt of the United
States has gone up another $10 billion. There is starvation; there is
homelessness; there is misery on every hand and corner, but mind
you, in the meantime, Mr. Roosevelt has had his way. He is one
man that can't blame any of his troubles on HUEY LONG. He has
had his way. Down in my part of the country if any man has the
measles he blames that on me; but there is one man that can't
blame anything on anybody but himself, and that is Mr. Franklin
De-La-No Roose-velt.

And now, on top of that, they order war on me because nearly 4
years ago I told Hoover's crowd it wouldn't do and because 3 years
ago I told Roosevelt and his crowd it wouldn't do. In other words,
they are in a rage at HUEY LONG because I have said, "I told you
so."

I am not overstating the conditions now prevailing in this country. In their own words they have confessed all I now say or ever
have said. Mr. Roosevelt and even Mrs. Roosevelt have bewailed
the fact that food, clothes, and shelter have not been provided for

the people. Even Gen. Hugh S. Johnson said in his speech of
Monday night that there are 80 million people in America who are
badly hurt or wrecked by this depression. Mr. Harry Hopkins,
who runs the relief work, says the dole roll has risen now to
22,375,000 persons, the highest it has ever been. And now, what is
there for the Roosevelt crowd to do but to admit the facts and
admit further that they are now on their third year, making matters worse instead of better all the time? No one is to blame,
except them, for what is going on because they have had their way.
And if they couldn't change the thing in over two years, now
bogged down worse than ever, how could anyone expect any good
of them hereafter? God save us two more years of the disaster we
have had under that gang.

Now, my friends, when this condition of distress and suffering
among so many millions of our people began to develop in the
Hoover administration, we knew then what the trouble was and
what we would have to do to correct it. I was the first man to say
publicly—but Mr. Roosevelt followed in my tracks a few months
later and said the same thing. We said that all of our trouble and
woe was due to the fact that too few of our people owned too much
of our wealth. We said that in our land, with too much to eat, and
too much to wear, and too many houses to live in, too many
automobiles to be sold, that the only trouble was that the people
suffered in the land of abundance because too few controlled the
money and the wealth and too many did not have money with
which to buy the things they needed for life and comfort.

So I said to the people of the United States in my speeches
which I delivered in the United States Senate in the early part of
1932 that the only way by which we could restore our people to
reasonable life and comfort was to limit the size of the big man's
fortune and guarantee some minimum to the fortune and comfort
of the little man's family.

I said then, as I have said since, that it was inhuman to have
food rotting, cotton and wool going to waste, houses empty, and at
the same time to have millions of our people starving, naked, and
homeless because they could not buy the things which other men
had and for which they had no use whatever. So we convinced Mr.
Franklin Delano Roosevelt that it was necessary that he announce
and promise to the American people that in the event he were
elected President of the United States he would pull down the size

of the big man's fortune and guarantee something to every family—enough to do away with all poverty and to give employment to those who were able to work and education to the children born into the world.

Mr. Roosevelt made those promises; he made them before he was nominated in the Chicago convention. He made them again before he was elected in November, and he went so far as to remake those promises after he was inaugurated President of the United States. And I thought for a day or two after he took the oath as President, that maybe he was going through with his promises. No heart was ever so saddened; no person's ambition was ever so blighted, as was mine when I came to the realization that the President of the United States was not going to undertake what he had said he would do, and what I know to be necessary if the people of America were ever saved from calamity and misery.

So now, my friends, I come to that point where I must in a few sentences describe to you just what was the cause of our trouble which became so serious in 1929, and which has been worse ever since. The wealth in the United States was three times as much in 1910 as it was in 1890, and yet the masses of our people owned less in 1910 than they did in 1890. In the year 1916 the condition had become so bad that a committee provided for by the Congress of the United States reported that 2 percent of the people in the United States owned 60 percent of the wealth in the country, and that 65 percent of the people owned less than 5 percent of the wealth. This report showed, however, that there was a middle class—some 33 percent of the people—who owned 35 percent of the wealth. This report went on to say that the trouble with the American people at that time was that too much of the wealth was in the hands of too few of the people, and recommended that something be done to correct the evil condition then existing.

It was at about the same time that many of our publications began to deplore the fact that so few people owned so much and that so many people owned so little. Among those commenting upon that situation was the *Saturday Evening Post,* which, in an issue of September 23, 1916, said: "Along one statistical line you can figure out a Nation bustling with wealth; along another a bloated plutocracy comprising 1 percent of the population lording it over a starveling horde with only a thin margin of merely well-to-do in between."

And it was, as the *Saturday Evening Post* and the committee appointed by Congress said, it was a deplorable thing back in 1916, when it was found that 2 percent of the people owned twice as much as all of the remainder of the people put together, and that 65 percent of all of our people owned practically nothing.

But what did we do to correct that condition? Instead of moving to take these big fortunes from the top and spreading them among the suffering people at the bottom, the financial masters of America moved in to take complete charge of the Government for fear our lawmakers might do something along that line.

And as a result, 14 years after the report of 1916, the Federal Trade Commission made a study to see how the wealth of this land was distributed, and did they find it still as bad as it was in 1916? They found it worse! They found that 1 percent of the people owned about 59 percent of the wealth, which was almost twice as bad as what was said to be an intolerable condition in 1916, when 2 percent of the people owned 60 percent of the wealth. And as a result of foreclosures, failures, and bankruptcies, which began to happen prior to and in the year of 1929, before the campaign of 1932, and at this late date, it is the estimate of all conservative statisticians that 75 percent of the people in the United States don't own anything, that is, not enough to pay their debts, and that 4 percent of the people, or maybe less than 4 percent of the people, own from 85 to 90 percent of all our wealth in the United States.

Remember, in 1916 there was a middle class—33 percent of the people—who owned 35 percent of the wealth. That middle class is practically gone today. It no longer exists. They have dropped into the ranks of the poor. The thriving man of independent business standing is fast fading. The corner grocery store is becoming a thing of the past. Concentrated chain-merchandise and banking systems have laid waste to all middle opportunity. That "thin margin of merely well-to-do in between" which the *Saturday Evening Post* mentioned on September 23, 1916, has dwindled to practically no margin of well-to-do in between. Those suffering on the bottom and the few lords of finance on the top are nearly all that are left.

It became apparent that the billionaires and multimillionaires even began to squeeze out the common millionaires, closing in and taking their properties and wrecking their businesses. And so we arrived (and are still there) at the place that in abundant America, where we have everything for which a human heart can pray, the hundreds of millions—or, as General Johnson says, the 80 million—of our people are crying in misery for the want of the things which they need for life, notwithstanding the fact that the country has had and can have more than the entire human race can consume.

The 125 million people of America have seated themselves at the barbecue table to consume the products which have been guaranteed to them by their Lord and Creator. There is provided by the Almighty what it takes for them all to eat; yea, more. There is provided more than what is needed for all to eat. But the financial masters of America have taken off the barbecue table 90 percent of the food placed thereon by God, through the labors of mankind, even before the feast begins, and there is left on that table to be eaten by 125 million people less than should be there for 10 million of them.

What has become of the remainder of those things placed on the table by the Lord for the use of us all? They are in the hands of the Morgans, the Rockefellers, the Mellons, the Baruches, the Bakers, the Astors, and the Vanderbilts—600 families at the most, either possessing or controlling the entire 90 percent of all that is in America. They cannot eat the food, they cannot wear the clothes, so they destroy it. They have it rotted; they plow it up; they pour it into the rivers; they bring destruction through the acts of mankind to let humanity suffer; to let humanity go naked; to let humanity go homeless, so that nothing may occur that will do harm to their vanity and to their greed. Like the dog in the manger, they command a wagonload of hay, which the dog would not allow the cow to eat, though he could not eat it himself.

So now, ladies and gentlemen, we come to that plan of mine for which I have been so roundly denounced and condemned by such men as Mr. Farley, Mr. Robinson, and Gen. Hugh S. Johnson, and other spellers and speakers and spoilers of the Roosevelt administration. It is for the redistribution of wealth and for guaranteeing comforts and conveniences to all humanity out of this abundance in our country. I hope none will be horror-stricken when they hear me say that we must limit the size of the big man's fortune in order to guarantee a minimum of fortune, life, and comfort to the little man; but, if you are, think first that such is the declaration on which Roosevelt rode into the nomination and election of President. While my urgings are declared by some to be the average of a madman, and by such men as General Johnson as insincere bait of a pied piper, if you will listen to me you will find that it is restating the laws handed down by God to man; you will find that it was the exact provision of the contract and law of the Pilgrim Fathers who landed at Plymouth in 1620.

Here's what the Pilgrim Fathers said in the contract with the early settlers in the year 1620. I read you article 5 from that contract: "5. That at ye end of ye 7. years, ye capital & profits, viz. the houses, lands, goods, and chatles, be equally devided betwixte ye adventurers, and planters; wch done, every man shall be free from other of them of any debt or detrimente concerning this adventure."

So the Pilgrim Fathers wrote into the covenant to do just exactly what the Bible said to do, that they should have an equal division of the wealth every seven years. I don't go that far; I merely advocate that no man be allowed to become so big that he makes paupers out of a million other people.

You will find that it is the cornerstone on which nearly every religion since the beginning of man has been founded. You will find that it was urged by Bacon, Milton, and Shakespeare in England, by Socrates, Plato, Theognis, and other wisest of men in Greece, by Pope Pius XI in the Vatican, by the world's greatest inventor, Marconi in Italy, by Daniel Webster, Ralph Waldo Emerson, Abraham Lincoln, Andrew Jackson, William Jennings Bryan, and Theodore Roosevelt in the United States, as well as by nearly all of the thousands of great men whose names are yet mentioned in history.

The principle was not only the mainspring of Roosevelt's nomination and election, but in the closing speech of Herbert Hoover at Madison Square Garden in November 1932, even Hoover said: "My conception of America is a land where men and women may walk in ordered liberty, where they may enjoy the advantages of wealth, not concentrated in the hands of a few but diffused through the lives of all."

And so now I come to give you again that plan, taken from these leaders of all times and from the Bible, for the sponsoring of which I am labeled America's menace, madman, pied piper, and demagogue.

I propose:

First. That every big fortune shall be cut down immediately by a capital levy tax to where no one will own more than a few million dollars, as a matter of fact, to where no one can very long own a fortune in excess of about three to four millions of dollars. I propose that the surplus of all the big fortunes, above the few millions to any one person at the most, shall go into the United States ownership. How would we get all these surplus fortunes into the United States Treasury? Not hard to do. We would not do it by making everyone sell what he owned; no. We would send everyone a questionnaire. On that he would list the properties he owns, lands and houses, stocks and bonds, factories and patents, and so on. Every man would place his appraisal on his property, which the Government would review and maybe change on some items. On that appraisal the big fortune holder would say out of what property he would retain the few millions allowed to him, the balance to go to the United States. Say Mr. Henry Ford should allow that he owned all the stock of the Ford Motor Co., worth, say, $2 billion; he could claim, say $4 million of the Ford stock, but $1,996,000,000 would go to the United States. Say the Rockefeller fortune was listed at $10 billion in oil stocks, bank stocks, money, and stores. Each Rockefeller could say whether he wanted his limit in either the money, oil, or bank stocks, but about nine billion and eight hundred million would go to the Government. And so, in this way, the Government of the United States would come into the possession of about two-fifths of its wealth, which on normal values would be worth, say, $165 billion.

Then we would turn to the inventories of the 25 million families of America. All those who showed properties and money clear of debts that were above $5,000 and up to the limit of a few millions would not be touched. But those showing less than $5,000 to the family free of debt would be added to, so that every family would start life again with homestead possessions of at least a home and the comforts needed for a home, including such things as a radio and an automobile. These things would go to every family as a homestead, not to be sold either for debts or taxes or even by consent of the owner except by the consent of the court or Government, and then only on condition that the court hold it to be spent for the purpose of buying another home and comforts thereof.

Such would mean that the $165 billion or more taken from big fortunes would have about $100 billion of it used to provide all with the comforts of home and living. The Government might have to issue warrants for claim and location, or even currency to be retired from such property as was claimed, but all that is a detail not impractical to get these homes into the hands of the people.

So America would start again with millionaires, but no multimillionaires or billionaires; with some poor, but none too poor to be denied the comforts of life. America, however, would still have maybe a $65 billion balance from these big fortunes not yet used to set up the poor people. What would we do with that? Wait a moment. I am coming to that, too.

Second. We propose that after homes and comforts of homes have been set up for the families of the country, that we shall turn our attention to the children and the youth of the land, providing first for their education and training. We would not have to worry about the problem of child labor, because the very first thing which we would place in front of every child would be not only a comfortable home during his early years but the opportunity for education and training, not only through the grammar school and the high school but through college and to include vocational and professional training for every child. If necessary, that would include the living cost of that child while he attended college, if one should be too distant for him to live at home and conveniently attend, as would be the case with many of those living in the rural areas.

We now have an educational system, and in States like Louisiana—and it is the best one—where school books are furnished free to every child and where transportation by bus is given to every student, however far he may live from a grammar or high school; there is a fairly good assurance of education through grammar and high school for the child whose father and mother have enough at home to feed and clothe them. But when it comes to a matter of college education, except in few cases the right to a college education is determined at this day and time by the financial ability of the father and mother to pay for the cost and the expense of a college education. It don't make any difference how brilliant a boy or girl may be, that don't give them the right to a college education in America today.

Now, Gen. Hugh Johnson says I am indeed a very smart demagogue, a wise and dangerous menace. But I am one of those who didn't have the opportunity to secure a college education or training. We propose that the right to education and the extent of education shall be determined and gauged not so much by the financial ability of the parents but by the mental ability and energy of a child to absorb the learning at a college. This should appeal to General Johnson, who says I am a smart man, since, had I enjoyed the learning and college training which my plan would provide for others, I might not have fallen into the path of the dangerous menace and demagogue that he has now found me to be.

Remember, we have $65 billion to account for that would lie in the hands of the United States, even after providing home comforts for all families. We will use a large part of it immediately to expand particularly the colleges and universities of this country. You would not know the great institutions like Yale, Harvard, and Louisiana State University. Get ready for a surprise. College enrollments would multiply 1,000 percent. We would immediately call in the architects and engineers, the idle professors and scholars of learning. We would send out a hurry call because the problem of providing college education for all of the youth would start a fusillade of employment which might suddenly and immediately make it possible for us to shorten the hours of labor, even as we contemplate in the balance of our program.

And how happy the youth of this land would be tomorrow morning if they knew instantly their right to a home and the comforts of a home and to complete college and professional training and education were assured! I know how happy they would be, because I know how I would have felt had such a message been delivered to my door.

I cannot deliver that promise to the youth of this land tonight, but I am doing my part. I am standing the blows; I am hearing the charges hurled at me from the four quarters of the country. It is the same fight which was made against me in Louisiana when I was undertaking to provide the free school books, free busses, university facilities, and things of that kind to educate the youth of that State as best I could. It is the same blare which I heard when I was undertaking to provide for the sick and the afflicted. When the youth of this land realizes what is meant and what is contemplated, the billingsgate and the profanity of all the Farleys and Johnsons in America can't prevent the light of truth from hurling itself in understandable letters against the dark canopy of the sky.

Now, when we have landed at the place where homes and com-

forts are provided for all families and complete education and
training for all young men and women, the next problem is what
about our income to sustain our people thereafter. How shall that
be arranged to guarantee all the fair share of what soul and body
need to sustain them conveniently. That brings us to our next
point. We propose:

No. 3. We shall shorten the hours of labor by law so much as
may be necessary that none will be worked too long and none
unemployed. We shall cut the hours of toil to 30 hours per week,
maybe less; we may cut the working year to 11 months' work and 1
month's vacation; maybe less. If our great improvement programs
show we need more labor than we may have, we will lengthen the
hours as convenience requires. At all events, the hours for production will be gauged to meet the market for consumption. We will
need all our machinery for many years, because we have much
public improvement to do; and, further, the more use that we may
make of them, the less toil will be required for all of us to survive
in splendor.

Now, a minimum earning would be established for any person
with a family to support. It would be such a living which one,
already owning a home, could maintain a family in comfort, of not
less than $2,500 per year to every family.

And now by reason of false statements made, particularly by
Mr. Arthur Brisbane* and Gen. Hugh S. Johnson, I must make
answer to show you that there is more than enough in this country
and more than enough raised and made every year to do what I
propose.

Mr. Brisbane says I am proposing to give every person $15,000
for a home and its comforts, and he says that would mean the
United States would have to be worth over a trillion dollars. Why
make that untrue statement, Mr. Brisbane? You know that is not
so. I do not propose any home and comfort of $15,000 to each
person—it is a minimum of $5,000 to every family, which would
be less than $125 billion, which is less than one-third of this Na-
tion's wealth in normal times of $400 billion.

General Johnson says that my proposal is for $5,000 guaranteed
earning to each family, which he says would cost from four to five
hundred millions of dollars per year, which he says is four times

*Arthur Brisbane, Hearst newspaper editor and writer.

more than our whole national income ever has been. Why make such untrue statements, General Johnson? Must you be a false witness to argue your point? I do not propose $5,000 income per year to each family. I propose a minimum of from $2,000 to $2,500 income per year to each family. For 25 million families that minimum income per family would require from $50 billion to $60.6 billion. In the prosperous days we have had nearly double that for income some years already, which allowed plenty for the affluent; but with the unheard prosperity we would have, if all our people could buy what they need, our national income would be double what it has ever been.

The Wall Street writer and statistician says we could have an income of at least $10,000 to every family in goods if all worked short hours and none were idle. According to him, only one-fourth of the average income would carry out my plan.

And now I come to the remainder of the plan. We propose:

No. 4. That agricultural production will be cared for in the manner specified in the Bible. We would plow under no crops; we would burn no corn; we would spill no milk into the river; we would shoot no hogs; would slaughter no cattle to be rotted. What we would do is this:

We would raise all the cotton that we could raise, all the corn that we could raise, and everything else that we could raise. Let us say, for example, that we raised more cotton than we could use.

But here again I wish to surprise you when I say that if everyone could buy all the towels, all the sheets, all the bedding, all the clothing, all the carpets, all the window curtains, and all of everything else he reasonably needs, America would consume 20 million bales of cotton per year without having to sell a bale to the foreign countries. The same would be true of the wheat crop, and of the corn crop, and of the meat crop. Whenever everyone could buy the things he desires to eat, there would be no great excess in any of those food supplies.

But for the sake of the argument, let us say, however, that there would be a surplus. And I hope there will be, because it will do the country good to have a big surplus. Let us take cotton as an example. Let us say that the United States will have a market for 10 million bales of cotton and that we raise 15 million bales of cotton. We will store 5 million bales in warehouses provided by the Government. If the next year we raise 15 million bales of cotton and only need 10, we will store another 5 million bales of cotton, and the Government will care for that. When we reach the year when we have enough cotton to last for twelve or eighteen months, we will plant no more cotton for that next year. The people will have their certificates of the Government which they can cash in for that year for the surplus, or if necessary, the Government can pay for the whole 15 million bales of cotton as it is produced every year; and when the year comes that we will raise no cotton, we will not leave the people idle and with nothing to do. That is the year when, in the cotton States, we will do our public improvement work that needs to be done so badly. We will care for the flood-control problems; we will extend the electricity lines into rural areas; we will widen roads and build more roads; and if we have a little time left, some of us can go back and attend a school for a few months and not only learn some of the things we have forgotten but we can learn some things that they have found out about that they didn't know anything about when we were children.

Now the example of what we would do about cotton is the same policy we would follow about all other crops. This program would necessitate the building of large storage plants, both heated and cold storage, and warehouses in all the counties of America, and that building program alone would take up all the idle people that America has today. But the money spent would go for good and would prevent any trouble happening in the future. And then there is another good thing. If we would fill these warehouses, then if there were to come a year of famine there would be enough on hand to feed and clothe the people of the Nation. It would be the part of good sense to keep a year or two of stock on hand all the time to provide for an emergency, maybe to provide for war or other calamity.

I give you the next step in our program:

No. 5: We will provide for old-age pensions for those who reach the age of 60 and pay it to all those who have an income of less than $1,000 per year or less than $10,000 in property or money. This would relieve from the ranks of labor those persons who press down the price for the use of their flesh and blood. Now the person who reaches the age of 60 would already have the comforts of home as well as something else guaranteed by reason of the redistribution that had been made of things. They would be given enough more to give them a reasonably comfortable existence in their declining days. However, such would not come from a sales tax or taxes placed upon the common run of people. It would be supported from the taxes levied on those with big incomes and the yearly tax that would be levied on big fortunes, so that they would always be kept down to a few million dollars to any one person.

No. 6. We propose that the obligations which this country owes to the veterans of its wars, including the soldiers' bonus and to care for those who have been either incapacitated or disabled, would be discharged without stint or unreasonable limit. I have always supported each and every bill that has had to do with the payment of the bonus due to the ex-service men. I have always opposed reducing the allowances which they have been granted. It is an unfair thing for a country to begin its economy while big fortunes exist by inflicting misery on those who have borne the burden of national defense.

Now, ladies and gentlemen, such is the share-our-wealth movement. What I have here stated to you will be found to be approved by the law of our Divine Maker. You will find it in the Book of Leviticus, from the twenty-fifth to the twenty-seventh chapters. You will find it in the writings of King Solomon. You will find it in the teachings of Christ. You will find it in the words of our great teachers and statesmen of all countries and of all times. If you care to write to me for such proof, I shall be glad to furnish it to you, free of expense, by mail.

Will you not organize a share-our-wealth society in your community tonight or tomorrow to place this plan into law? You need it; your people need it. Write me, wire to me; get into this work with us if you believe we are right. Help to save humanity. Help to save this country. If you wish a copy of this speech or a copy of any other speech I have made, write me and it will be forwarded to you. You can reach me always in Washington, D. C.

I thank you.

The St. Vitus' Dance Government

THE CONGRESSIONAL RECORD
May 7, 1935

MR. LONG. Mr. President, I ask unanimous consent to have a radio address printed in the RECORD.

MR. ROBINSON. What is the speech?

MR. LONG. A speech I made over the radio.

MR. ROBINSON. A speech the Senator himself made?

MR. LONG. Yes; a mighty good speech. [Laughter.]

MR. ROBINSON. It could not be a good speech if the Senator made it. [Laughter.] I shall not object to the request.

There being no objection, the address was ordered to be printed in the RECORD, as follows:

Radio address by Hon. Huey Long, of Louisiana, May 2, 1935

Ladies and gentlemen: Whether you do or do not believe in the divine rule of the Scriptures, or in the precepts of the founders of this country, or in history, or philosophy, if you will believe the four tables of arithmetic—those of addition, subtraction, multiplication, and division—you will agree with me that the wealth of this land must be immediately redistributed among our 125 million people if America is to be saved.

For a moment, ladies and gentlemen, let me turn to the last radio address delivered by our President, the Honorable Franklin

Delano Roosevelt. It was delivered to the people of our country on last Sunday night.

Now the President says that the people cannot understand just how good he has got them coming along. Here are his words: "The job of creating a program for the Nation's welfare is, in some respects, like the building of a ship. At different points on the coast where I often visit they build great sea-going ships."

You see what the President is talking about there, is that, when he goes out on that $5 million yacht they call the *Nourmahal,* owned by brother Vincent Astor, who does lots of ship-subsidy business with the United States, where they get as much as $1,000 for carrying a 3-cent letter, he sometimes sees them building ships. Now let us quote him further: "When one of these ships is under construction and the steel frames have been set in the keel, it is difficult for a person who does not know ships to tell how it will finally look when it is sailing the high seas. . . . It is that way with the making of a national policy."

Oh, so we see now, our President of the United States, the "Knight of the *Nourmahal,*" says we are confused because we cannot see just how this thing is going to look when he gets through making it. Why to be sure! All those millions of hogs they killed; all those cattle they shot down; the milk they poured into the rivers with the people starving for it; all of the cotton they plowed under and wool that they burned up, with the people naked because they could not get it; none of us can see just how that is working out. But the President says it is going to look pretty when he gets the picture made up. Surely it will look pretty. It may not look exactly like a song, but it will be something like a dance— the St. Vitus' dance.

Now, the President said this: "They know that the process of the constructive rebuilding of America cannot be done in a day or a year."

No; and if he is a fair sample of it, they know it cannot be done in 100 years. His process of construction, if you call it construction, is to start out repairing the automobile by first tearing off the top and then when the rain begins to beat in, to hammer the engine to pieces, tear down the chassis, and then wind up by taking off the wheels. That leaves only one thing to do—he sends the bill for the work. That bill has now reached the size of over $30 billion, six times more than all of the money in circulation in the United States.

But now we are getting to something. The President takes us into his confidence. Here is what he says next:

"The most difficult place in the world to get a clear and open perspective of the country as a whole is in Washington. . . . That is why I occasionally leave this scene of action for a few days to go fishing."

Now if you will observe closely, our President remarks that he could not find out about the people of the country in Washington, so he betook himself on board the $5 million yacht called the *Nourmahal*, owned by Vincent Astor, where he was dead certain to find out just how things were getting along. This *Nourmahal* yacht sailed out into the British waters with the President on board and soon thereafter was boarded by the son and daughter-in-law of the King of England, the Duke and Duchess of Kent, and now after some several days or weeks tour on the briny English waters, enthroned on a $5 million yacht, in company with the multimillionaire Astor and the Duke and Duchess of Kent right out of England, our great and benevolent President returns and says he went on this fishing trip to find out what it is all about.

This will be great comfort to the cotton hands who are not allowed to plant cotton this year. It will do a great deal of help among the starving who are told they must make contracts to reduce the quantity of foodstuffs so there will not be too much. Hooray for the President's fishing trip! Let's send him off again.

If he doesn't get any better understanding of conditions in this country than he has had in the last 2 years, it would be a fine thing if Congress made a contract with Mr. Vincent Astor and his $5 million yacht, not only to take the President out in the British waters to fish for a few weeks, but to keep him there for several more months and trust to luck the country would find its way back to normalcy.

I didn't get to hear the message of the President as it was delivered over the radio, because I was on board a train returning from Des Moines, where I had made a speech. But I will say to you that at that place I took a vote of the crowd—some 20,000 highly educated and intelligent people—and without one exception every hand was raised into the air favoring the plan for a redistribution of wealth and not one hand was raised against it.

But to get back to my point. Not having heard the President speak, as I returned to Washington I stepped over to my office when I was approached by an officer who said to me:

"I heard the President last night."

"What did he say?" I asked.

"He said to just keep waiting."

But the President of the United States has long since forgotten the pledge and promise which he made and on which he was nominated and elected the President of the United States. He promised in terms that were certain; in language which could not be misunderstood, that he would break up the size of the big fortunes of this country and use it to build the common people up from the ground to where they had something on which to live in comfort. He made that promise in the speech which he delivered in Atlanta, Ga., the basis on which I declared for him for President. He made that promise when he accepted the nomination of the Democratic Party at the Chicago convention. He made that promise in other speeches which he delivered during the campaign. And I was sent into State after State, directly from the then candidate for President—Mr. Roosevelt—to tell the people that when Mr. Franklin De-la-no Roosevelt became our President, that the big fortunes would be whittled down to a reasonable limit in size and that thereby the common run of mankind would be built up from the bottom, at least to the point where all our people had a home and the comforts of life for their families, with steady employment to all labor and profit over production costs to all farmers.

What I say as to these promises by our President will not be disputed by him or by anyone else. They are in indelible type; they are in letters and pamphlets that cannot be questioned.

But now, in the third year of his administration, we find more of our people unemployed than at any other time. We find our houses empty, our people hungry, many of them half clothed and many of them not clothed at all. We find not only the people going further into debt, but that the United States is going further into debt, the States are going further into debt, and the cities and towns are going even into bankruptcy. The condition has become deplorable. Instead of his promise, the only remedy that Mr. Roosevelt has prescribed is to borrow more money if we can and to go further into debt. The last move was to borrow $5 billion on which we must pay interest for the balance of our lifetime. And with it all there stalks the slimy specter of want, hunger, destitution, and pestilence, all because of the fact that in the land of too much to eat and too much to wear, our President has failed in his promise to have these necessities of life distributed into the hands of the people who have need of them.

Now the jet-black shadow of our want and misery came upon us step by step with certain precision, day after day, month after month and year after year. There were investigations and studies made both by private bodies and governmental agencies to find out the causes of our trouble. The whole matter was studied very seriously up to as late as the years 1916 to 1920. The departments of the United States Government and many of our statesmen and newspapers and other journals openly stated that our growing trouble was caused by too much of our wealth getting into the hands of too few of our people. All of them said that we had to turn things around the other way, so as to have the few people owning less and less; so as to have the masses own more and more.

But such things were said at a time before the money masters had muzzled these public journals and before they had stifled the agencies of our Government's research and publicity. Here is what the Government report rendered to Congress in 1916 by the Industrial Relations Commission said: "The sources from which industrial unrest springs are, when stated in full detail, almost numberless. But, upon careful analysis of their real character, they will be found to group themselves almost without exception under four main sources which include all the others. These four are:

"1. Unjust distribution of wealth and income."

The United States Industrial Relations Commission said further: "The rich, 2 percent of the people, own 60 percent of the wealth; the middle class, 33 percent of the people, own 35 percent of the wealth. The poor, 65 percent of the people, own 5 percent of the wealth. This means in brief that a little less than 2,000,000 people, who would make up a city smaller than Chicago, own 20 percent more of the Nation's wealth than all the other 90,000,000."

But at about the time these studies were being made, our country was thrown into the European war in 1917 and when the shades of 1919 were lowered on the peace conference in Paris, the billionaires and multimillionaires of our finances had begun to apply their pressure throughout America. They saw to it thereafter that nothing more was said about too few people owning too much, or about too many people owning too little. They muzzled down on everything as tight as a drum. From 1920 to 1929 they chained business and banks and roped in all of the businesses and institutions of this country four times as tight as they had ever held them. In the first year of Hoover's reign with more foodstuffs and more wearing apparel, more manufactured articles, more houses, and more of everything else than this country had ever seen in all of its history, notwithstanding all our abundance of everything for which our people had any need, there began to come about the first wave of our greatest hunger, nakedness, homelessness, and destitution in this land where there was too much of everything.

Why was that?

It was because of the fact that in spite of those conditions of too few owning too much, as we found to exist in 1916, that as a matter of fact in the 14 years time which followed from 1916 to 1930 those conditions grew to be two times as bad as they were when they were complained about in 1916. The study of the Federal Trade Commission, made in 1930, said:

"The foregoing table shows that about 1 percent of the estimated number of decedents owned about 59 percent of the estimated wealth and that more than 90 percent was owned by about 13 percent of this number."

So you will see from a comparison of these two Government reports that 1 percent of the people owned as much in 1930 as 2 percent of the people owned in 1916. So it proved that the Government was correct in 1916 when it warned that too much of the wealth in the hands of too few people was bringing on calamity; for when we reached 1930, with the condition growing from bad to worse, the whole country collapsed and misery was brought upon the population in the land that was flowing with milk and money.

From the studies which I made I charged along about the years 1932—33 on the floor of the United States Senate that 4 percent of the people owned 85 percent of the wealth and that 96 percent of our people owned less than 16 percent of the wealth. I charged that 70 percent of the people of the United States didn't own enough to pay their debts. There was considerable ridicule made against the figures which I gave. During the last month of April, of this very year, the newspaper in New York City with the largest circulation, the *Daily News,* announced that it would send a special representative to Washington to investigate the figures which I had given out. So it sent here a gentleman named Lowell Limpus, and in the issue

of the *Daily News* of Monday, April 8, 1935, just 8 weeks ago, here
is what that great newspaper said. I quote their words:

"Four percent own 87 percent of United States, *News* survey
shows."

Now, that is the headline of this newspaper. I will read you from
the article of this newspaper of April 8, 1935:

"The News recently suggested editorially that figures quoted in
current discussions on the distribution of wealth 'ought to be
proved or disapproved by an official survey.' No figures being
available, the News instituted a survey of its own. The results are
covered in a series of articles, of which this is the first."

Now I continue to quote from this article. Here is what they
said:

The News survey simply brings the picture up to date—or as
nearly so as figures permit. It reveals the following facts:

"Less than 4 percent are getting 38.5 percent of the aggregate
national income. They own and control more than 87 percent of
the national wealth.

"The poor are getting poorer. The national income is steadily
draining into fewer and fewer pockets. The Nation's wealth is
rapidly coming under the control of a mere handful of men."

I quote further from this article in the *Daily News*:

The facts were there, but they were ignored. It remained for
Senator HUEY LONG and his ilk to force them to the attention of
the public.

HUEY LONG OPENED BOOKS

He adopted a technique which had never occurred to the
students. Huey mounted a soap box and beat a bass drum. The
public stopped to listen. The News survey reveals that he knew
what he was talking about—but so did the students who pre-
ceded him.

So now, my friends, I will not take the time to read you further
what this big newspaper which checked up on my figures has said,
but it took the time to write an editorial, and here is what the
editorial of the New York *Daily News* of April 11, 1935, says:

When HUEY LONG in his share-the-wealth reply to General
Johnson said that 1 percent of Americans own 59 percent of

America's wealth, while 4 percent own between 85 percent and 95 percent of the wealth, we knew he was a liar. We intimated as much, and added that somebody ought to look into this question and get the true figures on American wealth distribution in order to refute this demagogue Long.

The News then assigned one of its most competent investigators, Lowell Limpus, to the job of digging up the figures. . . . And so Lowell Limpus went to Washington and worked for weeks in the Library of Congress and elsewhere to root up the true figures with which to confound Long.

The results of that research are now being published in the News. And to the consternation of many people (including ourselves when we first heard of them), the results of that research show that Long had essentially the correct dope.

The gist of the Limpus findings is this:

More than 96 percent of the workers in the United States receive less than the $2,000 a year which is regarded as "sufficient only for basic necessities."

According to the United States Federal Trade Commission, in 1926, 1 percent of the people dying did own 59 percent of the wealth reported; and since that time the rich have been getting richer in proportion and the poor poorer.

When Limpus discovered that such was the picture of wealth distribution in the United States he wired the News that his data would prove very startling, and that probably his findings could not be published.

It was decided, after some deliberation, to publish them nevertheless. That decision was made on the ground that the ostrich act of sticking our heads in the sand, blinding ourselves to facts will only do us harm in the long run. To suppress these facts might damper down some unrest for a while. But it is these facts which are causing the unrest. The eventual kick-back would be much more serious if the facts continued to be kept under cover.

And they are ominous facts. It has happened time and again that when a nation's wealth has become concentrated in too few hands, and ways of redistributing part of it peaceably have not been worked out, ways of redistributing it by violence have been adopted in time—as in France and Russia. And as long as mass purchasing power stays down and continues to shrink, there will be overproduction of the bathtubs, cars, radios, etc., which we like to think are elements in the American standard of living.

Will the balance of the newspapers do what this newspaper has done, or will they continue to be blind and lead the balance of the blind into the mire of destruction and ruin?

But the great journalistic thought of the present day refuses to see the light. The *Saturday Evening Post* of this week, dated May 4, 1935, has this leading editorial, from which I quote as follows:

FACTS ARE STUBBORN

Rarely does any subject receive so much attention as the Honorable HUEY LONG. There is grave discussion as to how he will affect the fortunes both of the new deal and of the Republican Party. . . . Everyone has an opinion as to whether he is a 'menace' or not; the view taken depending on many different factors. . . . The core of Senator LONG's plan is to take away from all persons such wealth as they have in excess of $1,000,000, giving them the right to choose what particular kinds of property they will keep within the maximum permitted. Of the total wealth thus appropriated, he suggests that something less than half be used to educate young people and that something over half be used to bring families having less than $5,000 of property up to that figure. . . . This country has no official figures or even accurate estimates concerning the distribution of wealth. All that can be done is to capitalize for estimate purposes the incomes reported by the Bureau of Internal Revenue, and on this basis, LONG's estimate of the wealth to be shared is 14 or 15 times too high.

I have not the time to read further from this editorial. You will see that it conflicts with two reports of the Government and the recent study made by the New York *Daily News,* to say nothing of my own calculations; but now note that this *Saturday Evening Post* article says that there are no figures to show the distribution of wealth. Because of that, I now ask you to let me read to you what this very same *Saturday Evening Post* said in its issue of September 23, 1916. That editorial is headed "Are We Rich or Poor?" And here is what the *Saturday Evening Post* itself said: "The man who studies wealth in the United States from statistics only will get nowhere with the subjects, because all the statistics afford only an inconclusive suggestion. Along one statistical line you can figure out a nation bustling with wealth; along another a bloated plutocracy comprising 1 percent of the population lording it over a starveling horde with only a thin margin of merely well-to-do in between."

What is the matter with you, *Saturday Evening Post?* Here you are saying there are no figures to show any such thing as I am saying, when nearly 20 years ago, when you were allowed to be honest, you told the people that 1 percent of the people had a stranglehold on nearly everything the country had in it. Why, this magazine doesn't know that I was its scholar in 1916 and it helped to push me along in this fight, and now, after 20 years of effort, it has failed to remember what it knew way back yonder and which everybody else has begun to find out at this late date.

So now, my friends, you have heard me read how a great New York newspaper, after investigation, has declared that all I have said about the bad distribution of this Nation's wealth is true. I have been severely condemned and ridiculed, over a period of many years, for persisting in giving the people the facts regarding this bad situation. Time after time, all that I have said has been pronounced false. Now they are beginning to say that it is all too true and too sad. I join them in their statements. It is too true and too sad. But we have been about our work to correct this situation. That is why the share-our-wealth societies are forming in every nook and corner of America. They are meeting tonight. Soon there will be share-our-wealth societies for everyone to meet. They have a great work to perform. Here is what we stand for, in a nutshell:

1. We propose that every family in America shall at least own a homestead equal in value to not less than one-third the average family wealth. The average family wealth of America, at normal values, is approximately $16,000. So our first proposition means that every family will have a home and the comforts of a home up to a value of not less than $5,000.

2. We propose that no family shall own more than 300 times the average family wealth, which means that no family shall possess more than a wealth of approximately $5 million. And we think that is too much. The two propositions together mean that no family

shall own less than one-third of the average family wealth, nor shall any family own more than 300 times the average-family wealth. That is to say that none should be so poor as to have less than one-third of the average, and none should be so rich as to have more than 300 times the average.

3. We next propose that every family shall have an income equal to at least one-third of the average family income in America. If all were allowed to work, according to our statistics, there would be an average family income of from $5,000 to $10,000 per year. So, therefore, in addition to the home which every family would own and the comforts of life which every family would enjoy, every family would make not less than $2,000 to $3,000 per year upon which to live and educate their children.

4. We propose that no family shall have an income of more than 300 times the average family income. Less the income taxes, this would mean an annual income of $1 million would be the maximum allowed to any one family in 1 year. The third and fourth propositions simply mean that no family should earn less than one-third the average, and no family should earn more than 300 times the average; none to make too much, none to make too little. Everyone to have the things required for life; every man a king.

5. We propose a pension to the old people. Under our proposal taxes would not be levied upon the sons and daughters, nor the working people to support their aged fathers and mothers. But on the contrary, such support as would be given for old-age pensions would be borne solely by the surplus money which the Government would rake off of the big fortunes and big inheritances.

6. We propose to care for the veterans of our wars, including the immediate cash payment of the soldiers' bonus, and last, but not least, we propose that every child in America shall have a right to education and training, not only through grammar and high school, but also through college and universities. And this education and training would be of such extent as will equip each child to battle on fair terms in the work which it is compelled to perform throughout life. We would not have it that a child could go to college or university provided his parents had the money on which to send him, but it would be the right of every child under our plan to the costs, including living expenses of college and university training, which could be done by our country at a cost considerably

less than is required for the military training which has been given
to the youth in the past.

My plan is that our Government should call in this surplus
wealth above a few million to any one family and then distribute it
out to those who have the need of the same. Some criticize that
plan, but it is prescribed by the Bible. I read you the words:

"And the multitude of them that believed were of one heart and
of one soul: neither said any of them that ought of the things which
he possessed was his own; but they had all things common.

"Neither was there any among them that lacked: for as many as
were possessors of lands or houses sold them, and brought the
prices of the things that were sold.

"And laid them down at the apostles' feet; and distribution was
made unto every man according as he had need." (See Acts, ch. 4,
verses 32–36.)

It is our purpose that every man should pursue a calling that
means a living to himself and his family in peace and comfort; that
the shelter and home of every family should be their own. That is
as the Bible says it should be. I read you the words:

"And they shall beat their swords into plowshares and their
spears into pruning hooks; nation shall not lift up a sword against
nation, neither shall they learn war any more, but they shall sit
every man under his vine and under his fig tree; and none shall
make them afraid" (Micah, ch. 4, verses 3 and 4).

We say that none shall be too rich and none too poor. The Bible
says such is as it should be. I read you the words: "Give me neither
poverty nor riches; feed me with food convenient for me; lest I be
full and deny Thee and say, 'Who is the Lord?' or lest I be poor
and steal, and take the name of my God in vain" (Proverbs, ch. 30,
verses 8 and 9).

And we say if these statutes of God are observed our people
shall live in peace and comfort forever. The Bible says so. I read
you the words: "If you walk in my statutes . . . ye shall eat your
bread to the full and dwell in your land safely, and I will give peace
in the land, and ye shall lie there and nothing should make you
afraid" (Leviticus, ch. 26, verses 3 to 17).

Let no one tell you that it is difficult to redistribute the wealth of
this land; it matters not how rich or great one may be, when he
dies his wealth must be distributed anyway. The law of God shows

how it has been done throughout time. Nothing is more sensible or better understood than the redistribution of property. The laws of God command it. It is required of all nations that live. (See Leviticus, ch. 26.) Today our Nation is cursed with an overload of debt; public and private debts aggregate $262 billion. That is more than $2,000 to every person. Under the present set-up this burden of debt can never be paid. It will forever condemn our people.

The laws of our Lord command that such burden of debt must be wiped out of existence so that a people may have a fair chance in life. (See Deuteronomy, ch. 15.)

So let us be about our work. It is simple. Why lie ye here idle? There is enough for all. Let there be peace in the land. Let our children be happy.

Our fight is now on here in the United States Senate to pay the soldiers' bonus. It is a debt which is due the soldiers who fought our wars. We are fighting to keep the Patman bill,* which actually pays this bonus, from being sidetracked. The bill is already past the House of Representatives. Maybe you would like to wire your United States Senator tonight to ask him to stand for the Patman bill tomorrow.

I would like to hear from any of you if you wish to concern yourself with the work that we have in hand. If you want a copy of my speech, I will send it upon request. You can write to me here in Washington, D. C., care of the United States Senate.

How wonderful, how great, how fruitful to all this great land of ours can be. We only have to eliminate useless greed, provide that none shall be too big and none too small. Beautiful America can rise to the opportunity before it. It means to us all:

Every man a king.

---

*Legislation to pay World War I veterans a special bonus, passed by Congress and vetoed by President Roosevelt.

A Fair Deal for the Veterans and The Share Our Wealth Principles

THE CONGRESSIONAL RECORD
May 23, 1935

MR. LONG subsequently said: Mr. President, I ask to have inserted in the RECORD, at the close of my speech on the veto message, an address and a letter which I send to the desk.

There being no objection, the address and the letter were ordered to be printed in the RECORD, as follows:

Address By Senator Huey P. Long, of Louisiana, Entitled "A Fair Deal For the Veterans", Made Over a National Broadcasting Co. Network, Saturday Night, May 11, 1935, Under the Auspices of The Veterans of Foreign Wars

The Congress of the United States, by an overwhelming majority in both Houses, has voted to pay in full what is generally called the "soldiers' bonus," but what, in reality, is not a soldiers' bonus at all, but the adjusted-service wages—and very poor wages, at that—which the Government allowed to the soldiers for the days that they served in the World War.

We have generally referred to this proposition as the soldiers' bonus. But here is what it was:

When the boys came back from the war in 1918 and 1919, and some as late as 1920, the Government said that since all common labor had been paid from $3 to $4 per day during the war, without taking any chance of being shot down, or of having their legs shot off, or their eyes shot out, that they would pay the soldiers for the time that they worked, fought, and risked their lives and bodies the same amount per day as the commonest kind of laborer was paid for the same day's work during the war.

Now, since they figured that the soldier had already been paid around $30 to $40 per month while he was in the war, they deducted the $1 or $1.25 per day, and gave him a certificate for the balance, so that, when his certificate was paid, the soldier would receive as much money for the days that he stood in the trenches as the commonest kind of laborer received for the same days that he worked.

Now, I think you or I or most any other person would say that, as a general rule, the man who worked and fought, who slept in the trenches, on the ground, in the rain, and in the mud, and who took a chance of never coming back, was entitled to get a little bit more money for that kind of service than the man who lived in comfort in his home, and took no such chance of being maimed or killed.

But we did not regard it that way when we gave the soldiers their certificates for service. We took the view that they were not entitled to any more money than the sorriest kind of field hand, or work hand; and that is the certificate which they hold today, which is called the soldiers' bonus.

A few years ago Congress provided that the soldiers could borrow about half the money that was due on their certificates. Now, what we have done here this week is to provide to pay them the balance, equal to the face value of the certificates issued by the Government for their services. Some people talk as though the soldiers had already been paid one bonus. That is not true at all. We have not paid the soldiers the bonus once, or twice, or anything of the kind. What we did was to issue a certificate to each man, giving him an allowance to be paid later, and we have allowed them to borrow on this certificate up to one-half the face value, but we have never paid the obligation at all. That is what we are trying to do now.

Now we propose, and have passed a law, to pay the amount in full. The law which has been passed is known as the Patman bill. It is the same bill that previously passed the House of Representatives. Last year I offered this bill as an amendment to another bill in the United States Senate. It failed to pass. But in this session of Congress this same Patman bill was voted in the House of Representatives by an overwhelming majority. It came to the Senate, and it was voted there by a very large majority.

It will become the law, if the President signs it. But, even though the President vetoes the bill it will become the law anyway, if two thirds of the United States Senators will vote to override the President's veto. We are very near to the mark of getting two thirds of the Senators to vote to override the veto. It is a shame to have a few votes help the President to sustain a veto doing this wrong to the men who fought our battles.

That being the case, every person, whether he has or has not written to the President, should immediately write or wire to his United States Senators, asking them to vote to override the veto on the soldiers' bonus bill in case he vetoes the bill. We hear the President is being urged to turn a deaf ear to the people's plea. Therefore, wire your Senators.

Now, the President tells us that he was a veteran of the World War, too, and that he understands it somewhat better than we may think. Well, it is true that Mr. Roosevelt was a veteran of the World War. He was Assistant Secretary of the Navy. He stayed up here on Pennsylvania Avenue in the daytime, and in a very fine home during the nighttime, and he drew $10,000, a year for his services. He was 3,000 miles away from gunfire. Of course, he had an income besides that, which made him say that he did not need the $10,000 but we paid him that, anyway. And nobody is trying to take it away from him.

But the man that he does not seem to have learned about, is the man that did not stay on Pennsylvania Avenue, and who did not stay in any luxurious home, but the man who scoured the seas, who walked and slept in the rain, who stood in the mud waist deep in the trenches, who went over the top and faced the German guns, who breathed the poisonous gases, and who not only went through fourteen kinds of carnage worse than the fires of hell itself, but who, when he came back, found his occupation destroyed, and the job which he had held gone.

But Mr. Roosevelt forgets that his pay of $10,000 per year was ten to twenty times the amount which we are trying to get for the soldier who crossed the seas, who faced the enemy, and probably came back home not half fit to live. Someone said to me that some soldiers they knew ought not to be paid the bonus because they had turned out to be bums. Who was it that made them bums? The Government sent them into the fires of death and I wonder that as many came out as well as they did. That's no argument against paying the bonus.

And Mr. Roosevelt forgets, further, that he got his $10,000 right on the barrel-head for every day that he worked or did not work, and enjoyed Washington society to the full limit in the meantime; whereas the soldier has now waited seventeen years for his money, and they are still fighting to keep him from having it.

I am somewhat in the position of Mr. Roosevelt on the war. He didn't go and I didn't go. The only difference is that I didn't get $10,000 a year not to go. If he wants to place me in his status, all he has to do is to send me a check for $5,000 for every year the war went on and we will be 50–50 on the war—neither ever heard a cap snap and both with $5,000 per year, instead of him with the whole $10,000 by himself.

It is true that he advocated going into the war and I advocated not going into the war. I was against the war, and now so is everybody else who has seen how we came out; but, outside of that, the only thing that keeps me from being the same kind of soldier that Mr. Roosevelt was is that I did not get any $10,000 and I did not try to make anybody else go to war.

Now, the Government of the United States has issued its certificate for this money to every one of these soldiers. It is due and required to be paid in the year 1945; that, is ten years from now. What we have done in Congress and in the United States Senate by the Patman bill is to provide that the soldier can put up this Government certificate and get Government currency, of Government money, for an amount that is equal to the face value of the service certificate, just like they allow bankers to draw face value in money on obligations of the Government which they hold.

In other words, let us say that the soldier holds a service certificate for $500. Under our bill he could put up that certificate and the Government would pay him $500 in cash. There is nothing new about that. Everybody else that holds a Government bond or certificate can put it up and get the Government money on it. Right today a bank can take any bond or obligation that it has of the United States, and put that bond up and draw the money in cash on the bond—and that doesn't half tell the story.

Not only can the bank draw the money on the bond that it has, but they can draw the interest on the bond, notwithstanding the fact that they have drawn the money on it; and when the bond becomes due they will have drawn interest all the time, and still have had all the money all the time to do with just as they desired.

Nearly every Member in the Congress, and nearly every Member in the United States Senate, has voted at least three times within the last 3 years to allow the bankers to take the bonds and obligations of the United States Government and put them up with the Treasury Department and secure as much money on the bonds as the face value of the bonds represented, and then the bonds stood there, in their name, and they could draw the interest until their maturity date, and never pay out a cent of their money in the meantime.

But they are not willing to do half that good by the soldier. All that the soldier is asking to do, under the Patman bonus bill, is to put up his adjusted-service certificate, and, if it is for $500, that he be given $500 of Treasury notes, which is the same kind of paper money that you have in your pocket today, if you have any. The soldier would not get any interest on his service certificate, like the banks do on the bonds and obligations that they put up to get money, and the only thing today that we have to decide, is: Will we say to the soldier with the $500 bond, "No, we won't let you have the $500 in money"; and then turn around to the bankers, who have a million dollars' worth of bonds, and say, "We not only will give you the $1 million in paper money for your $1 million of bonds, but we will also pay you 4 percent interest on the bonds until the date of their payment arrives."

Why on March 9, 1933, 5 days after Mr. Franklin Delano Roosevelt took the office as President of the United States, we had another one of these bills up, and we passed it, allowing all banks to put up the bonds of the Government, and to get circulating money, dollar for dollar, and allowing them to draw their interest, just the same, while they had the money. Why didn't Mr. Roosevelt veto that?

Now, the argument has been made that to issue these soldiers this money is opening up the printing press to print money. This is a very flimsy pretense, particularly when Mr. Roosevelt has signed two bills to print all the money that the bankers wanted issued for their bonds.

There is today in the United States Treasury $9 billion in gold. As against that gold, we have only five and one-half billions of dollars in money in the United States. If we issue the money on every one of these adjusted-service-certificate bonds held by the soldiers and sailors, we would only pay out around $2 billion, which means that, with the money we now have outstanding, and the other money that we would have outstanding, we would have in circulation money of all kinds amounting to about seven and one-half billions, and, as against that seven and one-half billions, we would have over $9 billion in the Treasury in gold alone, to say nothing of the silver, with which to pay off the money on demand.

But the people are not allowed to ask for their money in gold today. Your paper money says on the face of it that you have a right to demand its payment in gold at the Treasury; but we have another law which says that if you go there to get the money in gold that you would be put in jail for getting it. So where is Mr. Roosevelt to stand when he vetoes the soldier's right to cash his service-certificate bond?

But even if we were on a gold standard, who could say that we would be issuing printing-press money? Our sound gold law only requires 40 cents in gold in the United States Treasury to back up a dollar of outstanding paper money. That would mean that the United States Government today, with the $9 billion in gold it has, could issue up to 22½ billions of dollars in paper currency, and still be on the soundest kind of gold standard based upon the gold reserve of nine billions that we have in the Treasury; and there would not be any inflation about it. Yet they stand against us having Government money to pay off the soldiers, when we would have only 7½ billion dollars in money covered by $9 billion in gold, or $1.20 in gold for every paper dollar that was outstanding after paying the bonus.

The soldier is entitled to be paid this bonus; he has done his work; he has made his fight; he has taken his chance; he has made his sacrifice; he has kept the faith; and he is the only one who never was paid the daily wage for the days he worked during the war. No one has been more badly treated than the average man who risked his life in the service of this country, to be paid the lowest wages of all, on the chance of losing his life, and then wait seventeen years and still not have the low wages he was promised.

Maybe we cannot get the President of the United States to see it, but the bankers have been given everything for which they have asked, and if they have been allowed to put up their bonds and get money on them, and still draw interest on the bonds, at the very least we ought to let the soldier put up his certificate and be paid money on it, when he is not allowed interest, as the banker has been allowed.

It is hard to understand how the President could have framed himself into a mind that opposes paying his obligation which the Government now owes to the soldiers. The other night, in his speech over the radio, he said that because he could not find out the touch of the American people, he sometimes went out fishing on the *Nourmahal* yacht of Vincent Astor, so as to get a better conception of the feeling of the American people. I am afraid that his sailing on that $5 million yacht, into the British waters, where he visited with the Duke and Duchess of Kent, the son and daughter-in-law of King George the Fifth and Queen Mary, the four-fifths, has distorted the viewpoint of the President, rather than giving him the common perspective of the common people in this country.

I hope that he will pay attention to the letters and telegrams which he is receiving, and judge that as being nearer the impression of the American people, rather than the views of the high aristocracy with which he surrounded himself upon the late pleasant cruise into the British waters.

Wire your United States Senators now, or, if you do not feel like spending the money to wire, then write them a letter. Ask them to put their shoulders to the wheel to help override the veto of the President. Do not take any chances. Ask them to do the same justice by the soldiers as has been done by the captains of finance.

Great good would be done this country if we paid this two and one-quarter billion dollars into the channels of our commerce. It would stimulate business everywhere. It would do the people more good than it would the soldiers.

In truth and in fact, we are simply asking that the soldier now be paid, after 17 years of waiting, the commonest kind of wages which others were paid during the time when he fought in the trenches.

Wire your Senators! Wire your Senators!

The Share Our Wealth Principles

(Senator Huey P. Long's letter)

THE SHARE OUR WEALTH PRINCIPLE—ROOSEVELT PROMISED TO FULFILL THEM—HOOVER DECLARED THEM HIS CONCEPTION OF AMERICA—

BUT ONLY ORGANIZED SOCIETIES CAN FORCE THE KEEPING OF SUCH
PLEDGES —THE LAW OF THE BIBLE—THE COMPACT OF THE PILGRIMS IN
1620—THE GUARANTY OF THE DECLARATION OF INDEPENDENCE—THE
BASIS FOR OUR CONSTITUTION—AMERICA'S ONLY SALVATION—"HE WHO
FALLS IN THIS FIGHT FALLS IN THE RADIANCE OF THE FUTURE!"

(The share-our-wealth society proposes to enforce the traditions
on which this country was founded, rather than to have them
harmed; we aim to carry out the guaranties of our immortal Declaration of Independence and our Constitution of the United States,
as interpreted by our forefathers who wrote them and who gave
them to us; we will make the works and compacts of the pilgrim
fathers, taken from the Laws of God, from which we were warned
never to depart, breathe into our Government again that spirit of
liberty, justice, and mercy which they inspired in our founders in
the days when they gave life and hope to our country. God has
beckoned fullness and peace to our land; our forefathers have set
the guide stakes so that none need fail to share in this abundance.
Will we now have our generation, and the generations which are to
come, cheated of such heritage because of the greed and control of
wealth and opportunity by 600 families?)

To members and well-wishers of the share-our-wealth society:
    For twenty years I have been in the battle to provide that, so
long as America has, or can produce, an abundance of the things
which make life comfortable and happy, that none should own so
much of the things which he does not need and cannot use as to
deprive the balance of the people of a reasonable proportion of the
necessities and conveniences of life. The whole line of my political
thought has always been that America must face the time when the
whole country would shoulder the obligation which it owes to
every child born on earth—that is, a fair chance to life, liberty, and
happiness.
    I had been in the United States Senate only a few days when I
began my effort to make the battle for a distribution of wealth
among all the people a national issue for the coming elections. On
July 2, 1932, pursuant to a promise made, I heard Franklin Delano
Roosevelt, accepting the nomination of the Democratic Party at
the Chicago convention for President of the United States, use the
following words: "Throughout the Nation, men and women, forgotten in the political philosophy of the Government for the last

years, look to us here for guidance and for a more equitable opportunity to share in the distribution of the national wealth."

It therefore seemed that all we had to do was to elect our candidate and that then my object in public life would be accomplished.

But a few nights before the Presidential election I listened to
Mr. Herbert Hoover deliver his speech in Madison Square
Garden, and he used these words: "My conception of America is a
land where men and women may walk in ordered liberty, where
they may enjoy the advantages of wealth, not concentrated in the
hands of a few, but diffused through the lives of all."

So it seems that so popular had become the demand for a redistribution of wealth in America that Mr. Hoover had been compelled to somewhat yield to that for which Mr. Roosevelt had
previously declared without reservation.

It is not out of place for me to say that the support which I
brought to Mr. Roosevelt to secure his nomination and election as
President—and without which it was hardly probable he would
ever have been nominated—was on the assurances which I had
that he would take the proper stand for the redistribution of
wealth in the campaign. He did that much in the campaign; but
after his election, what then? I need not tell you the story. We
have not time to cry over our disappointments, over promises
which others did not keep, and over pledges which were broken.

We have not a moment to lose.

It was after my disappointment over the Roosevelt policy, after
he became President, that I saw the light. I soon began to understand that, regardless of what we had been promised, our only
chance of securing the fulfillment of such pledges was to organize
the men and women of the United States so that they were a force
capable of action, and capable of requiring such a policy from the
lawmakers and from the President after they took office. That was
the beginning of the share-our-wealth society movement.

Let me say to the members and well-wishers that in this movement, the principles of which have received the endorsement of
every leader of this time, and of other times, I am not concerned
over my personal position or political fortune; I am only interested
in the success of the cause; and on any day or at any time when, by
our going for any person or for any party, we can better, or more
surely or more quickly secure home, comfort, education, and happiness for our people, that there is no ambition of mine which will

stand in the way. But there can be no minimum of success until every child in this land is fed, clothed, and housed comfortably and made happy with opportunity for education and a chance in life.

Even after the present President of the United States had thrown down the pledge which he had made time after time, and rather indicated the desire, instead, to have all the common people of America fed from a half-starvation dole, while the plutocrats of the United States were allowed to wax richer and richer, even after that, I made the public proposition that if he would return to his promise and carry out the pledge given to the people and to me that, regardless of all that had passed, I would again support his administration to the limit of my ability.

Of course, however, I was not blind; I had long since come to the understanding that he was chained to other purposes and to other interests which made impossible his keeping the words which he uttered to the people.

I delayed using this form of call to the members and well-wishers of the share-our-wealth society until we had progressed so far as to convince me that we could succeed either before or in the next national election of November 1936. Until I became certain that the spirit of the people could be aroused throughout the United States, and that, without any money—because I have none, except such little as I am given—the people could be persuaded to perfect organizations throughout the counties and communities of the country. I did not want to give false hopes to any of those engaged with me in this noble work. But I have seen and checked back enough, based upon the experiences which I have had in my public career, to know that we can, with much more ease, win the present fight, either between now and the next national campaign, or else in the next national campaign—I say with much more ease than many other battles which I have won in the past but which did not mean near so much.

We now have enough societies and enough members, to say nothing of the well-wishers, who—if they will put their shoulders to the wheel and give us one-half of the time which they do not need for anything else—can force the principles of the share-our-wealth society to the forefront, to where no person participating in national affairs can ignore them further.

Now, here is what I ask the officers and members and well-wishers of all the share-our-wealth societies to do—two things to wit:

First. If you have a share-our-wealth society in your neighbor-hood—or, if you have not one, organize one—meet regularly, and let all members, men and women, go to work as quickly and as hard as they can to get every person in the neighborhood to be-come a member and to go out with them to get more members for the society. If members do not want to go into the society already organized in their community, let them organize another society. We must have them as members in the movement, so that, by having their cooperation, on short notice we can all act as one person for the one object and purpose of providing that in the land of plenty there shall be comfort for all. The organized 600 families who control the wealth of America have been able to keep the 125 million people in bondage because they have never once known how to effectually strike for their fair demands.

Second. Get a number of members of the Share Our Wealth Society to immediately go into all other neighborhoods of your county and into the neighborhoods of the adjoining counties, so as to get the people in the other communities and in the other counties to organize more Share Our Wealth Societies there; that will mean we can soon get about the work of perfecting a com-plete, unified organization that will not only hear promises but will compel the fulfillment of pledges made to the people.

It is impossible for the United States to preserve itself as a republic or as a democracy when 600 families own more of this Nation's wealth—in fact, twice as much—as all the balance of the people put together. Ninety-six percent of our people live below the poverty line, while 4 percent own 87 percent of the wealth. America can have enough for all to live in comfort and still permit millionaires to own more than they can ever spend and to have more than they can ever use; but America cannot allow the multi-millionaires and the billionaires, a mere handful of them, to own everything unless we are willing to inflict starvation upon 125,000,000 people.

We looked upon the year 1929 as the year when too much was produced for the people to consume. We were told, and we be-lieved, that the farmers raised too much cotton and wool for the people to wear and too much food for the people to eat. There-fore, much of it went to waste, some rotted, and much of it was burned or thrown into the river or into the ocean. But, when we picked up the bulletin of the Department of Agriculture for that year 1929, we found that, according to the diet which they said everyone should eat in order to be healthy, multiplying it by 120 million, the number of people we had in 1929, had all of our people had the things which the Government said they should eat in order to live well, we did not have enough even in 1929 to feed the people. In fact, these statistics show that in some instances we had from one-third to one-half less than the people needed, particularly of milk, eggs, butter, and dried fruits.

But why in the year 1929 did it appear we had too much? Because the people could not buy the things they wanted to eat, and needed to eat. That showed the need for and duty of the Government then and there, to have forced a sharing of our wealth, and a redistribution, and Roosevelt was elected on the pledge to do that very thing.

But what was done? Cotton was plowed under the ground. Hogs and cattle were burned by the millions. The same was done to wheat and corn, and farmers were paid starvation money not to raise and not to plant because of the fact that we did not want so much because of people having no money with which to buy. Less and less was produced, when already there was less produced than the people needed if they ate what the Government said they needed to sustain life. God forgive those rulers who burned hogs, threw milk in the river, and plowed under cotton while little children cried for meat and milk and something to put on their naked backs!

But the good God who placed this race on earth did not leave us without an understanding of how to meet such problems: nor did the pilgrim fathers who landed at Plymouth in 1620 fail to set an example as to how a country and a nation of people should act under such circumstances, and our great statesmen like Thomas Jefferson, Daniel Webster, Abraham Lincoln, Theodore Roosevelt, and Ralph Waldo Emerson did not fail to explain the need and necessity for following the precedents and purposes, which are necessary, even in a land of abundance, if all the people are to share the fruits produced therein. God's law commanded that the wealth of the country should be redistributed ever so often, so that none should become too rich and none should become too poor; it commanded that debts should be canceled and released ever so often, so that the human race would not be loaded with a burden which it could never pay. When the Pilgrims landed at Plymouth in

1620, they established their law by compact, signed by everyone who was on board the *Mayflower,* and it provided that at the end of every seven years the finances of their newly founded country would be readjusted and that all debts would be released and property redistributed, so that none should starve in the land of plenty, and none should have an abundance of more than he needed. These principles were preserved in the Declaration of Independence, signed in 1776, and in our Constitution. Our great statesmen, such men as James Madison, who wrote the Constitution of the United States, and Daniel Webster, its greatest exponent, admonished the generations of America to come that they must never forget to require the redistribution of wealth if they desired that their Republic should live.

And, now, what of America? Will we allow the political sports, the high heelers, the wiseacres, and those who ridicule us in our misery and poverty to keep us from organizing these societies in every hamlet so that they may bring back to life this law and custom of God and of this country? Is there a man or woman with a child born on the earth, or who expects ever to have a child born on earth, who is willing to have it raised under the present-day practices of piracy, where it comes into life burdened with debt, condemned to a system of slavery by which the sweat of its brow throughout its existence must go to satisfy the vanity and the luxury of a leisurely few, who can never be made to see that they are destroying the root and branch of the greatest country ever to have risen? Our country is calling; the laws of the Lord are calling; the graves of our forefathers would open today if their occupants could see the bloom and flower of their creation withering and dying because the greed of the financial masters of this country has starved and withheld from mankind those things produced by his own labor. To hell with the ridicule of the wise street-corner politician. Pay no attention to any newspaper or magazine that has sold its columns to perpetuate this crime against the people of America. Save this country. Save mankind. Who can be wrong in such a work, and who cares what consequences may come following the mandates of the Lord, of the Pilgrims, of Jefferson, Webster, and Lincoln? He who falls in this fight falls in the radiance of the future. Better to make this fight and lose than to be a party to a system that strangles humanity.

It took the genius of labor and the lives of all Americans to produce the wealth of this land. If any man, or 100 men, wind up with all that has been produced by 120 million people, that does not mean that those 100 men produced the wealth of the country; it means that those 100 men stole, directly or indirectly, what 125 million people produced. Let no one tell you that the money masters made this country. They did no such thing. Very few of them ever hewed the forest; very few hacked a crosstie; very few ever nailed a board; fewer of them ever laid a brick. Their fortunes came from manipulated finance, control of government, rigging of markets, the spider webs that have grabbed all businesses; they grab the fruits of the land, the conveniences and the luxuries that are intended for 125 million people, and run their heelers to our meetings to set up the cry, "We earned it honestly." The Lord says they did no such thing. The voices of our forefathers say they did no such thing. In this land of abundance, they have no right to impose starvation, misery, and pestilence for the purpose of vaunting their own pride and greed.

Whenever any newspaper or person, whether he be a private individual or an officer of the Government, says that our effort to limit the size of fortunes is contrary to the principles of our Government, he is too ignorant to deserve attention. Either he knows that what he says is untrue or else he is too ignorant to know what the truth is.

We can go further than that: Whenever any person says that he is following any Christian religion; or, if he be a Jew, if he says he is following the religion of the Jews; or even if he be a Chinaman, if he is following the teachings of Confucius, he cannot say that he thinks his own religion is sound unless he is willing to follow the principles to share the wealth of the land. Such is taught and required in the lines of the Bible, both in the New Testament and in the Old Testament, and the divine warning of those pages, repeated time and again, is that unless there is a comfortable living guaranteed to the man at the bottom, and unless the size of the big man's fortune is so limited as to allow the common run of people a fair share of the earth's fruits and blessings, that a race of people cannot survive.

If a man declare himself to be an American, and a believer in the American principles, then from the day that this country was founded until the present time, whether it be by the French or by the English, he must profess the share-our-wealth principles, or else he is not following the American doctrine. When the Pilgrims landed at Plymouth, here was a part of their compact and law: "5. That at ye end of ye 7 years, ye capital & profits, viz., the houses, lands, goods, and chatles, be equally devided betwixte ye adventurers, and planters; who done, every man shall be free from other of them of any debt or detrimente concerning this adventure."

When the Declaration of Independence was written in 1776, here was a part of that immortal document:

We hold these truths to be self evident, that all men are created equal, that they are endowed by their Creator with certain inalienable rights, that among these are life, liberty, and the pursuit of happiness. That to secure these rights (of life, liberty, and happiness), governments are instituted among them, deriving their power from the consent of the governed. That whenever any form of government becomes destructive of these ends (of life, liberty, and happiness), it is the right of the people to alter or to abolish it; and to institute new government, laying its foundation on such principles and organizing its power in such form, as to them shall seem most likely to effect their safety and happiness.

When James Madison, the father of the Constitution of this country, looked over the situation, here is what he said: "We are free today substantially, but the day will come when our Republic will be an impossibility. It will be an impossibility because wealth will be concentrated in the hands of a few. A republic cannot stand upon bayonets, and when that day comes, when the wealth of the Nation will be in the hands of a few, then we must rely upon the wisdom of the best elements in the country to adjust the laws of the Nation to the changed conditions."

When the greatest exponent of our Constitution and of our Union, Daniel Webster, spoke of this principle, he said this:

The freest government, if it could exist, would not be long acceptable if the tendencies of the law were to create a rapid accumulation of property in few hands and to render the great mass of the population dependent. Universal suffrage, for example, could not long exist in a community where there was a great inequality of property. In the nature of things, those who have not property and see their neighbors possess much more than they think them to need cannot be favorable to laws made for the protection of property.

And so, even if this principle born of the Creator when he placed the first man on earth, reaffirmed by Christ and the Apostles, and which was made a part of this country from the day that the Pilgrims first landed, is now to be cast aside, if it is to be misrepresented by some of the newspapers and magazines and by bought-out politicians and hired perverters of the truth, none the less the common run of mankind cannot escape the calamity unless the wealth of our land is distributed. To see men, politicians, and journals engaged in a business to betray mankind, to spread untruths and ridicule so that men and women may be lowered into the turmoil of distress, misery, and death; to see people with talent willing to sell their genius and to use their efforts to curse and destroy their fellow beings, is almost inconceivable in the sight of God and man. Nevertheless, the greatest institution of America today is that concerted group of multimillionaire and billionaire families, whose organization has written "liar" across the heart of men of ability, of whom they make use to thwart justice, equity, and mercy among mankind.

We are calling upon people whose souls cannot be cankered by the lure of wealth and corruption. We are calling upon people who have at heart, above their own nefarious possessions, the welfare of this country and of its humanity. We are calling upon them, we are calling upon you, we are calling upon the people of America, upon the men and women who love this country, and who would save their children and their neighbors from calamity and distress, to call in the people whom they know, to acquaint them with the purposes of this society and secure organization and cooperation among everyone willing to lend his hand to this worthy work. Fear of ridicule? Fear of reprisal? Fear of being taken off of the starvation dole? It is too late for our people to have such fears. I have undergone them all. There is nothing under the canopy of heaven which has not been sent to ridicule and embarrass my efforts in this work. And yet, despite such ridicule, face to face in any argument I have yet to see the one of them who dares to gainsay the principle of our wealth. On the contrary, when their feet are put to the fire, each and every one of them declare that they are in favor of sharing the wealth, and the redistribution of wealth. But then some get suddenly ignorant and say they do not know how to do it. Oh, ye of little faith! God told them how. Apparently they are too lazy in mind or body to want to learn, so long as their ignorance is for the benefit of the 600 ruling families of America who have forged chains of slavery around the wrists and ankles of 125 million free-born citizens. Lincoln freed the black man, but today the white and the black are shackled far worse than any colored person in 1860.

The debt structure alone has condemned the American people to bondage worse than the Egyptians ever forged upon the Israelites. Right now America's debts, public and private, are $262 billion, and nearly all of it has been laid on the shoulders of those who have nothing. It is a debt of more than $2,000 to every man, woman, or child. They can never pay it. They never have paid such debts. No one expects them to pay it. But such is the new form of slavery imposed upon the civilization of America; and the street-corner sports and hired political tricksters, with the newspapers whom they have perverted, undertake to laugh, to scorn the efforts of the people to throw off this yoke and bondage; but we were told to do so by the Lord, we were told to do so by the Pilgrim Fathers, we were guaranteed such should be done by our Declaration of Independence and by the Constitution of the United States.

Here is the whole sum and substance of the share-our-wealth movement:

1. Every family to be furnished by the Government a homestead allowance, free of debt, of not less than one-third the average family wealth of the country, which means, at the lowest, that every family shall have the reasonable comforts of life up to a value of from $5,000 to $6,000. No person to have a fortune of more than 100 to 300 times the average family fortune, which means that the limit to fortunes is between $1½ and $5 million, with annual capital levy taxes imposed on all above $1 million.

2. The yearly income of every family shall not be less than one-third of the average family income, which means that, according to the estimates of the statisticians of the United States Government and Wall Street, no family's annual income would be less than from $2,000 to $2,500. No yearly income shall be allowed to any person larger than from 100 to 300 times the size of the average family income, which means that no person would be allowed

to earn in any year more than from $600,000 to $1,800,000, all to be subject to present income-tax laws.

3. To limit or regulate the hours of work to such an extent as to prevent overproduction; the most modern and efficient machinery would be encouraged, so that as much would be produced as possible so as to satisfy all demands of the people, but to also allow the maximum time to all workers for recreation, convenience, education, and luxuries of life.

4. An old-age pension to the persons over 60.

5. To balance agricultural production with what can be consumed according to the laws of God, which includes the preserving and storage of surplus commodities to be paid for and held by the Government for the emergencies when such are needed. Please bear in mind, however, that when the people of America have had money to buy things they needed, we have never had a surplus of any commodity. This plan of God does not call for destroying any of the things raised to eat or wear, nor does it countenance wholesale destruction of hogs, cattle, or milk.

6. To pay the veterans of our wars what we owe them and to care for their disabled.

7. Education and training for all children to be equal in opportunity in all schools, colleges, universities, and other institutions for training in the professions and vocations of life; to be regulated on the capacity of children to learn, and not on the ability of parents to pay the costs. Training for life's work to be as much universal and thorough for all walks in life as has been the training in the arts of killing.

8. The raising of revenue and taxes for the support of this program to come from the reduction of swollen fortunes from the top, as well as for the support of public works to give employment whenever there may be any slackening necessary in private enterprise.

I now ask those who read this circular to help us at once in this work of giving life and happiness to our people—not a starvation dole upon which someone may live in misery from week to week. Before this miserable system of wreckage has destroyed the life germ of respect and culture in our American people let us save what was here, merely by having none too poor and none too rich. The theory of the share-our-wealth society is to have enough for all, but not to have one with so much that less than enough remains for the balance of the people.

Please, therefore, let me ask you who read this document—please help this work before it is too late for us to be of help to our people. We ask you now, (1) help to get your neighbor into the work of this society and (2) help get other share-our-wealth societies started in your county and in adjoining counties and get them to go out to organize other societies.

To print and mail out this circular costs about 60 cents per hundred, or $6 per thousand. Anyone who reads this who wants more circulars of this kind to use in the work, can get them for that price by sending the money to me, and I will pay the printer for him. Better still, if you can have this circular reprinted in your own town or city.

Let everyone who feels he wishes to help in our work start right out and go ahead. One man or woman is as important as any other. Take up the fight! Do not wait for someone else to tell you what to do. There are no high lights in this effort. We have no State managers and no city managers. Everyone can take up the work, and as many societies can be organized as there are people to organize them. One is the same as another. The reward and compensation is the salvation of humanity. Fear no opposition. "He who falls in this fight falls in the radiance of the future!"

Yours sincerely,

Huey P. Long,
United States Senator, Washington, D. C.

To: Huey P. Long,
    U. S. Senator,
    Washington, D. C.

This is to inform you that a Share Our Wealth Society has been organized here with _ _ _ _ _ _ members. Address and officers are as follows:

Post office: _ _ _ _ _ _ _ _ _ _ _ _ _ _ _ _   State _ _ _ _ _ _
President: _
Address: _
Secretary: _
Address: _

(Allied Printing Trades Council, Union Label, Baltimore, 5.)

The Need of Truth and Sincerity in Mr. Roosevelt's Promises

THE CONGRESSIONAL RECORD
July 22, 1935

MR. LONG. Mr. President, I ask unanimous consent to have printed in the RECORD a radio speech delivered by me on Friday evening last.

There being no objection, the speech was ordered to be printed in the RECORD, as follows:

The Need of Truth and Sincerity in Mr. Roosevelt's Promises

It has been more than 3 years since the Democratic Party nominated Franklin Delano Roosevelt for President. It will soon be 3 years since he was elected President. He has served as our President during nearly all of 1933, during all of 1934, and during the year 1935 up to this date. When he has served that length of time he has made clear to the American people what might be expected of him.

When Mr. Roosevelt took the reins of affairs he immediately started in a direction exactly opposite to what he had promised the people. To my surprise, the leaders of the Democratic Party, and, for that matter, the leaders of all other parties, said, "Let him have his way. The people want him to have a chance." I answered them and said, "But this is different from what the people were promised. They were promised something else, and they have a right to have the President and the Congress live up to our platform and to the promises of the President."

I need not tell you the result. Our course of conduct in government has been such as Mr. Roosevelt wanted it to be. He has had his way. He has had a larger majority of Congressmen with him than any other President ever had. He has had the largest majority that any President has ever had in the United States Senate. Whatever he has wanted to be done has been done; whatever he has not wanted to be done has not been done.

On various occasions Mr. Roosevelt has decided that he has not wanted the Congress to act like Congress at all, but that he would like to have the Congress pass over to him their rights and functions as lawmakers, and the Congress has done that, time after time. In fact, they have resigned so many of their own duties and functions and given their powers over to the President that they ought to be ashamed to draw their money as lawmakers any longer. If you hire me to cut a cord of wood and instead of cutting the cord of wood some man comes along and says that I don't know how to cut that wood, but ought to let him cut it, and I hand him over the saw and the axe, then you ought to pay the man that cuts the wood and not pay me for the work. So when the people elected Senators and Congressmen to make laws and they took their seats in the Capitol, and Mr. Roosevelt walked up and said, "Here, you boys; you ain't fit to make any laws; let me do that for you," and we turned over the lawmaking authority to him, then we ought to have got up and left and not charged the people anything for our work.

We have in this country what is known as a "relief roll." Before they began to politicize it, it was supposed to put every man who had nothing to do on the relief and pay him a little something because he had nothing to do. When the Senators and Representatives in Congress voted all their affairs into the hands of Mr. Roosevelt, they ought to immediately have been put on the dole roll, instead of being allowed to draw $10,000 a year apiece to do nothing.

Now, it so happened that when Mr. Roosevelt stepped out and began to exercise these lawmaking powers, and to make rules and impose taxes and levy tributes and make rewards under them, they finally got up to the United States Supreme Court, and there and then the United States Supreme Court said that the Constitution of the United States had provided for the people to elect a Congress to make laws, and that there were such things in this country as forty-eight sovereign states. So the Supreme Court said further that the Senators and Representatives in Congress did not have a right to give away their own power to make the laws, and much less did they have the right to give away the right of the forty-eight states to run themselves as they were supposed to do. And a terrible squal went up from the White House.

I do not know whether the Supreme Court has acted in time to save the American Republic, but I feel certain that they have acted none too quickly. If this country lasts twenty years longer, we will owe it to the Supreme Court of the United States.

Now, let us review some of the things Mr. Roosevelt said he was going to do, and what he has done: The first thing he promised was to abolish the bureaucratic system of government. He said these bureaus and commissions that were being set up in Washington by Hoover and other Presidents were contrary to the American system, and were tangling up the people's business to where they did not know how to handle it. But what did he do when he got in office? He set up so many bureaus that they could not even give them names. They had to designate them by three and four letters in the alphabet. Then he wore the alphabet out and had to begin to use the numerals. Right today I am a Member of the United States Senate, a lawyer of twenty years' experience, served as Governor of the State of Louisiana for four years, and as a member of the public service commission of my State for ten years. I am right here in Washington, and I don't know the names or the duties of 1 percent of the boards and commissions that Roosevelt has set up since he has been President, and what is more, Roosevelt doesn't know them either.

Without any authority whatever from the state governments, they have set these bureaus up to run the states; they are putting departments of education in some of the states; they are putting departments for public works in some of the states; they are setting up their own spending agencies in the states. None of this kind of function is authorized in the Constitution of the United States. They can only be done through the authority of the State, if done constitutionally, but states will have to go to the Supreme Court of the United States to stop the illegal spending of money in such States in a wanton and reckless manner, and demand the rights of the states to carry on their functions in an orderly way. Louisiana will lead off with a suit of this kind in October. It will probably be followed by suits in many of the other states.

The NRA is now as dead as a door nail, but they kept it alive so that they could keep all the job holders on the rolls. The AAA has been held unconstitutional by many of the courts. Only today they tried to pass in the United States Senate a law to prevent any taxpayer from collecting money that had been illegally taken from him under the processing taxes. We managed to vote that down. Notwithstanding these decisions of the Supreme Court of the United States—and they are very sound and proper decisions—the Congress is being told to go right ahead and pass more unconstitutional laws, and after they have passed these unconstitutional laws they bulldoze and browbeat the people for two or three years before the courts can set them aside. Then, after that is done, they come in and ask Congress to pass a law forbidding anybody to sue for the harm that has been done to them under these unconstitutional laws.

There was never known such a high-handed, tyrannical, outrageous system of government since the days of Nero, or during the days of Nero, as has been perpetrated by this outlandish system of Roosevelt's brain-trust-bureaucratic-alphabetical conglomeration of everything except sense and justice.

Now, let us look at a few of the results. First, let us look at unemployment. Today, according to figures given to me by the American Federation of Labor, there are 734,000 more unemployed working people than there were for the same month last year. This same labor board says that there are around 11 million unemployed industrial workers in this country today. If we will take the figures to show what agriculture is making and compare it with a normal year, we will come to the conclusion that the agricultural workers are at least one-half unemployed, which would add about 10 million more people to the unemployed list. At any rate, the highest unemployment that has ever been known in this country exists right today under Roosevelt. Notwithstanding the fact that our people are unemployed and having nothing to do, we have now got down to the point to where we are not making enough of the necessities of life in this country for the people to live on. With our farmers and our working people and our business men standing by idle, much of the meat which we eat, many of the clothes which we wear, some of the shoes that we put on our feet, and even the cottonseed oil that is consumed in this country are brought here from foreign countries. Some of the countries that formerly bought their cotton from America, and their corn and their wheat from America, are now sending the same products that they used to buy from us back here to sell to us, and they have got things so rigged up and messed up in Washington that the men and women who want to raise these things and make these things are starving to death and still cannot get a job.

With all these conditions, nonetheless in three years of Roosevelt administration they have spent more money than all the Presidents of the United States spent put together, from George Washington to Woodrow Wilson. In 124 years, from the time George Washington began as President until Woodrow Wilson became President, we spent slightly over $24 billion. That covered all the wars, including the War of 1812, the Civil War, and the Panama Canal. But Mr. Roosevelt's administration has spent 24 billions in 3 years, as much as they spent in 124 years, and still we are worse off than we ever were, and we have had no war.

I have before me figures to show that in the city of New York, where all the money has been spent, and where, I am told, they even found some of the policemen on the relief rolls, there were 4,200 children who failed to attend school, who gave as their reason that they did not have any money with which to buy clothes so that they could go to school. For the last four months the pay rolls in this country have dropped every month. March was worse than February, April was worse than March, and May was worse than April. The "brain trusting" Government under Roosevelt went out to make some experiments to find out what was the matter. They wanted to find out why more people did not own their homes. What do you think they found out? They came back and made the remarkable report that after surveying forty-three states and spending several millions of dollars, they had come to the conclusion that the reason that people did not own more homes and better homes was because they did not have money to buy them. If that gang of nitwits gets farther away from Washington, and if they don't watch out, they will arrest them and put them in a zoo. They had better stay here where they are recognized, and where they know they are running the country. The sane people out in the open spaces may not find it out before it is too late.

You know, when they built the Panama Canal during Theodore Roosevelt's time—you might refer to Theodore Roosevelt as "Roosevelt the Great," and, in order to distinguish one of these Roosevelts from the other, we ought to refer to this Franklin Delano Roosevelt as "Roosevelt the Little," but to get back to the point—during Theodore Roosevelt's time we said a whole lot about his building the Panama Canal, about what a terrible extravagance it was. Well, the Panama Canal cost $525 million. That was a lot of money. But every month Mr. Franklin Delano Roosevelt throws away $570 million, which means that every month Roosevelt the Little spends $45 million more money than it cost Roosevelt the Great for the whole Panama Canal.

The national income has fallen from around 100 billions down to 42 billions under Roosevelt the Little, but while the income has fallen the debts have mounted higher and higher, and taxes have gone higher and higher. Public debts and the private debts amount to $262 billion. The interest on the debts owed in the United States, and taxes paid by the people of the United States, together amount to $28 billion per year. Just think of it! The whole national income is 42 billions, and 28 billions of it went for interest on debts and taxes, leaving only 14 billions out of the entire 42 billions that was not taken out by the Government or charged off for interest before people got started.

There have been some people who have fared rather well from this national calamity, if it were not for the fact that the big house is going to be pulled down on them, along with the balance of us, before they get through. As an example, Mr. Vincent Astor and his partners, the men that own this *Nourmahal* yacht, where they take the President out on his fishing trips—a five-million-dollar palace that floats out on the sea—these men had themselves a shipping outfit; they bought some ships from the United States Government, or, rather, I should say the United States Government had paid them some money to get them to take the ships and obligate themselves to run the *Leviathan*. The time came when Mr. Astor and his partners did not want to run the *Leviathan*, so they got into default with the United States by not running the *Leviathan*, and owed Uncle Sam $1,720,000. There was an individual over in the Department of Commerce by the name of Mitchell, who was Assistant Secretary of Commerce. The first thing he knew, the President had them release Astor from this contract to pay the $1,720,000, on the condition that Astor's crowd would build another ship that the Government would lend them nearly all the money to build, and that the Government would give them a mail contract so that they could not do anything but make more money. What it amounted to was that Astor's crowd not only were relieved of paying the $1,720,000 they owed the Government, but they were given something for the permission of the Government relieving them.

Mitchell wrote a letter to the President complaining about it, and he was instantly dismissed. They offered him a better job rather than to dismiss him if they could quiet him down and move him out of the way in time, but he would not stand for it, so he has been made to appear as a terrible character, and that has been what they have done with every man who has yelled about these frauds.

A while back here I submitted affidavits, reports from Government agents, and everything else to show what [James A.] Farley had been doing. I, as a Member of the United States Senate, asked for an investigation of Farley's conduct. I saw no reason why they should not investigate him, they having investigated me on five or six separate occasions. Notwithstanding all the exposures, they voted to keep Farley from being investigated.

The other day they wanted to investigate some people who came to lobby in Washington, and they had no hesitancy in appropriating several thousands of dollars to start investigating them right at once. But to investigate the inside of what was going on under Farley was something that could not be brought to light; they would have none of it, and they did not.

Now, you have been reading about the row that has been going on between the national administration and the State of Louisiana because of the fact that I am opposed to the way Mr. Roosevelt and his "brain trusters" and bureaucrats are running things. Louisiana does not propose to have itself put into bondage forever like some of these other States may want to do. Louisiana is a sovereign State, and our people insist upon being free men and women. They elect their officers, and they serve subject to the will of those people. But from here in Washington Mr. Roosevelt and his bureaucrats and autocrats have decided that they will take over the affairs of Louisiana. They undertook to send reputed political characters into that State to run our business; and they say, "Either we will run it this way or we will not run it at all." Our answer to them is that the people of Louisiana will run our State, and that we will not countenance the usurpation of the functions that the Constitution gives to a sovereign State. Our people will remain free.

The Federal Government says that they will not lend Louisiana any money out of the public-works funds. Well, if Louisiana borrowed any of their money we would have to give the bonds and obligations of the State, or of some subdivision of the State, to get it. If we need any money we do not have to get it that way. We can sell the bonds of the State of Louisiana on the open market without asking the Federal Government to lend us any of the PWA money. We did that yesterday. Louisiana bonds sold for $3.80 above par. When the United States Government wants to get money for its bonds it has to compel the banks to take them. That is where the Government bonds are today—in the bank vaults. If they did not buy them the banks would be out of business. Louisiana bonds are saleable on the open market without anyone being coerced to buy them. Why? Because Louisiana is a solvent and a well-run State. It takes in more money than it spends. The Federal Government spends $5 where it takes in $2. Our State bonds are far better than the Government bonds. I might say to the people of this State that you have heard a great deal of Louisiana. It is time that you should know more about it. I became Governor of that State in 1928. We had around, maybe, as much as 50 miles of paved highway when I took the helm of the State. At this time we have 3,500 miles of paved highways in Louisiana. We have, to add to that, some 10,000 more miles of farmer's graveled roads. When I became Governor of that State the census showed that it had 238,000 illiterate adults. That number was very quickly cut in half. It was my administration which gave the State free school books to all the school children. Before our time there were no bridges over the big rivers and streams. They had to be crossed on ferries at a cost of all the way from 50 cents to $2. Today, over those same rivers and streams you will find the large, long, and fine bridges we built, and you cross them absolutely without cost. They are free to the traveling public.

Before our time—I mean by that, before Governor Allen* and myself were factors in the State—our State university had an enrollment of 1,500; it now has 5,500. Its status has risen under us from class C to class A. We have built a new medical college, graded class A by the American Medical Association and to it we are now adding a large new college of dentistry. We are laying plans now so that every poor boy in Louisiana will be able to get a college education. We intend to have our plan working by September 1936, so that those who cannot pay all will pay what they can, and so that those who can pay none will nevertheless be given employment at our State university, so that they can have an opportunity to pursue a college course of education or instruction.

It might be well that you people who have heard of Louisiana should know that when I became Governor of that State the hospitals for mental diseases were overcrowded; some persons suffering with afflictions of the mind were incarcerated in jail cells, waiting for someone to die to make room for them in the hospital. I have broadened, enlarged, and improved those hospitals in Louisiana so that no longer are there people in the jail cells waiting for treatment, but today there is room in those institutions to care for additional people, and their standards have been improved.

The years before I became the Governor of the State, and before Governor Allen's time, the penitentiary lost as much as $1,000,000 a year in its operations, but now, under Governor Allen and during the last year of my term, the penitentiary is on a self-sustaining and paying basis.

You find in Louisiana a people enjoying all these improvements; you find there the State universities; you find there that the public schools are now largely supported from the State treasury; you find there that the State university, which was given $800,000 a year before I became Governor, is now drawing $2,750,000 per year to carry on its work of education. Yet with it all, you will find that the taxes in Louisiana have been reduced on all property, and now we have voted laws by which, this year, most of our home owners will be relieved from paying any taxes at all on their homes and others will be given back a large part of the taxes which they pay on their homes.

With such great improvements, accompanied by such tax reduc-

*Governor Oscar K. Allen, Long's hand-picked successor.

tions on properties, there is only one other thing that you should notice, and that is that Louisiana is a solvent State with a balanced budget, spending less than it takes in. It has several millions of dollars for the treasury to use for tax-relief purposes this winter. Therefore, that sovereign State and its people will not be subdued or humiliated with the demands and orders of bureaucrats and tin-pot tyrants in Washington, who never have been elected to anything, who never will be elected to anything, and who are taking billions of dollars of the people's money to gobble up in the political practices which they are now using for the ruination of this country.

And now, my friends, this brings me to the last part of my speech. Out of this orgy of chaos, out of this dreary atmosphere of calamity and confusion, what is our hope and our port of safety and security? It will be found in the promise of the President of the United States when he accepted the nomination at the Chicago convention. Prior to the Chicago convention I was the sole author of a plan known as the share-our-wealth plan. It proposed that none should own too much, and none should own too little. It necessarily required a redistribution of wealth, so that those who had more than they had any business with, should be made to give over to the Government the money and things which the Government would furnish to the people who did not have enough upon which to live. I proposed that plan when I became a member of the United States Senate early in 1932. It would do this: No man would be permitted to own more than a few millions of dollars, and no family would be allowed to have less than a home and reasonable other things so as to live in comfort. No man would have been allowed to make more than from several hundred thousand dollars up to a million dollars in 1 year. No family would have been allowed to earn less than from $2,000 to $2,500 per year. The rule is that no man should own more than or make more than 100 times what the average family owned or made, and that no family should own or make less than one-third what the average family owned or made. The further provision was that those persons who reached the age of 60 should be given an adequate pension of somewhere around $30 to $40 per month, unless they owned considerable property or had a livable income. Also, my plan contemplated the full payment of the debt to soldiers; and, finally, the guarantee from the Government of education, even through college, to all children for professional or vocational service in life. No boy or girl would have wanted for the desired education or training in college on account of the poverty of the family. Such was my plan.

It became known as the "share our wealth" plan in later days. Before Mr. Roosevelt was nominated, I had seen to it that he had committed himself to this principle, in the main, and that he had promised to commit himself after his nomination. And so, at the Chicago convention, he appeared and made this pledge, which I quote from his speech:

"Throughout the Nation men and women, forgotten in the political philosophy of the Government of the last years, look to us here for guidance and for more equitable opportunity to share in the distribution of national wealth."

So, ladies and gentlemen, you might now say, as was said before Mr. Roosevelt's election, that he pledged himself to the Huey Long share-our-wealth plan. Since Mr. Roosevelt has taken the office of President, he has opposed every effort to adopt the plan for redistribution of wealth. Time and again I have offered this plan to the Congress. I have offered the old-age pension plan; his administration has caused its defeat. I have offered the plan to pay the soldiers what we owe them; he has caused its defeat. I have offered the plan to educate the children in colleges; he has caused its defeat. I have offered the plan by which all would be assured of homes, and of incomes sufficient to keep them in comfort, and he has caused its defeat.

But lo and behold, with the public roused from coast to coast, and from the Canadian line to the Gulf, Mr. Roosevelt decided that he had to make a gesture the other day. It was the fifth time he had made the gesture, but he made it again. He sent a message to Congress saying that he was for the "share our wealth" plan. Immediately I called upon him to assist in passing a bill. What has he done? He sent us a bill already—that is, a bill has come up there, but they have been hiding it ever since—providing for taxes on big fortunes, which they said would yield $340 million a year. As a matter of fact, it would not yield half that much, but at best their claims were that it would yield $340 million a year. That was not even to be paid out to the people; it was to go on the deficit of the Government. The entire $340 million per year, if it had been that much, and it was not, would have been one-tenth of the annual deficit of Roosevelt's administration. If it had not gone on the deficit it would have given everybody $2.70 a year. In other words, he declared for share our wealth and sent us a bill to Congress that was as much like the share-our-wealth plan as a bedbug is like a hotel. And that is about the kind of fodder we get from him every time.

Take the way he gummed up the old-age pension plan we had. I proposed in Congress to give the people who were 60 years old or older from $30 to $40 per month, unless they had an income of $1,000 a year, or unless they owned $10,000 worth of property. He came in with a plan proposing as if he were going to have a genuine old-age-pension plan for the United States. It appropriated $49 million a year out of the United States Treasury and provided that the States had to match the $49 million, so as to make a total of $98 million. There were over 14 million people in the United States over 60 years old who were entitled to the pension under my plan. The whole $49 million of the Government, and the whole $49,000,000 of the States, the entire $98 million, would have given them all about $7 a year apiece. And that is just the kind of way the Roosevelt administration has deluded and gummed up and blind-sighted the people of the United States ever since he started out.

I have no faith whatever in the pledges of this administration. Some days ago they made the announcement that they had sent $1,700,000 to Louisiana to the university there. I warned those people that they had not done any such thing, and that they never would do it. Today they admit themselves that they did not send it, and do not intend to send it.

Such a Government, such lack of dependability, such lack of integrity—the Roosevelt administration—the St. Vitus dance government of the United States of America.

But our hope lies in the ultimate victory for the share-our-wealth plan, none would have too much, but all would have enough.

But although Mr. Roosevelt has refused to let the share-our-wealth bill become a law, yet the fact that he says what I say and prays for the share-our-wealth plan at least puts him on record to where no man who claims to be for Roosevelt can say other than that "Huey Long is right." They say that Mr. Roosevelt has only done this so as to steal my political thunder, or to take the wind out of my sails. Call it a mere imitation of my talk, if you will; call Mr. Roosevelt's gesture for the share-our-wealth plan a counterfeit, if you desire; the fact remains that no one imitates another imitation, and no one counterfeits another counterfeit. If Mr. Roosevelt considers that either HUEY LONG or his share-our-wealth plan is so popular or so good that he must either imitate or counterfeit it for his own sake, then he knows that the genuine plan is considered sound enough, good enough, and popular enough to justify his imitation or counterfeit. In all events, you who would take the word or gesture of Roosevelt, must do honor and add prestige and dignity to the share-our-wealth cause, however insincere Mr. Roosevelt may be.

I ask everyone to join in this move that will mean success to the share-our-wealth plan, and thereby life, liberty, and happiness to all our people.

Index